ROOTS OUT OF DRY GROUND

THE MOTHER REATHA HERNDON STORY

DORIS J. SIMS, PH.D.

ROOTS OUT OF DRY GROUND

THE MOTHER REATHA HERNDON STORY

WELSTAR PUBLICATIONS

Roots Out of Dry Ground

Written by Doris J. Sims, Ph.D.
Published by Welstar Publications, LL.C.
Horace Batson, Publisher
628 Lexington Avenue, Brooklyn, NY 11221.
Phone: (646) 409-0340
Fax: (313) 453-6554
E-mail: publisher@welstarpublications.com
or drbatson@optonline.net
ISBN: 978-0-938503-24-8

Managing Editor: Dr. Joanne Noel
Associate Editor: Mrs. Shiqeerah Ebanks
Book Design/Typography: Lori Monroe
Text set in Book Antigua
Cover Design: Lori Monroe

Dedication

This book is dedicated to all evangelists, pastors, and missionaries, who have labored, sacrificed, and unselfishly given their lives for the sake of the gospel, so that souls would be saved, delivered and set free.

Table of Contents

Bishop Charles Edward Blake Sr.,
Presiding Bishop for the Church of God in Christ, Inc.

Special Tribute to Mother Reatha Herndon

It gives me great joy to pay tribute to Mother Reatha Herndon. Mother Herndon was a powerful, anointed, and spirit-filled woman of God with an unparalleled legacy. Her story is awe-inspiring and full of the power of God. Her story deserves to be told.

Mother Herndon started out on the path of evangelism as a young woman and was later appointed as the first National Elect Lady of the Evangelist Department by the Second National Supervisor of Women, Mother Lillian Coffey. Mother Herndon was chosen to represent the women in the

National Evangelist Department who were working with Bishop Lucius C. Page. She served as head of the department for over 50 years.

Reatha and her twin sister, Leatha, were heralded and recognized for the work that they had accomplished in evangelizing, both near and far. They were trailblazers-going into areas where no Church of God in Christ had ever existed, sleeping in the same tent where they ministered, and preaching under brush arbors and on street corners, in the cities and in the country. They preached in the sunshine, rain and snow. They fearlessly went into these areas and established numerous churches throughout the nation. They embodied the true essence of the Great Commission of Jesus Christ which says in Matthew 28:19, "Go ye therefore, and teach all nations, baptizing them in the name of the Father, and of the Son, and of the Holy Ghost."

This powerful duo was instrumental in establishing over 75 churches, nursing them in their infancy until a pastor could be appointed. Many of those churches still exist today. These true servants of God sacrificed their own comforts and personal wellbeing for the gospel. Mother Herndon, along with her sister, brought many souls into the kingdom who became bishops, pastors, missionaries, deacons and grounded laypersons. The kingdom of God truly grew under Reatha and Leatha's leadership. Their lives and ministry embody the work of an evangelist.

Leatha passed away in the 70's, however, that did not stop Mother Herndon. She continued to minister and preach the word of God. She worked relentlessly for the kingdom until she passed away in 2005 at 104 years old. Mother Herndon gave her life to the ministry of Jesus Christ and the Church of God in Christ. No task was too lowly or mundane. Mother Herndon's willingness to serve without regard for compensation or remuneration shows her total dedication to evangelism. As you read about this great pioneer, may you be inspired to serve as she served, work as she worked, and sacrifice as she sacrificed. Mother Herndon was truly a bright light in the Church of God in Christ history. The flame of evangelism will never go out.

Your Servant in Christ,

Bishop Charles E. Blake Sr.,

The Seventh in Succession
The Presiding Bishop
The Church of God in Christ, Inc.

MOTHER WILLIE MAE RIVERS,
GENERAL SUPERVISOR OF WOMEN INTERNATIONAL

SPECIAL ACKNOWLEDGEMENT

It is my delight to acknowledge the contributions of Mother Reatha Herndon and her sister, Leatha. The Church of God in Christ has been tremendously blessed by their ministry. I know of no other persons in the Church of God in Christ who can attest to "preaching out" over 75 churches, running thousands of revivals and bringing countless souls to Christ, other than Mother Herndon and her sister, Leatha.

Mother Herndon embodies the true concept of evangelism. She was more than a missionary; she established her name as an evangelist that touched the lives of many. Mother Herndon also played a tremendous role in helping to lay the foundation of the International Women's Department.

She was a wonderful example and a true blessing to all of the women. Neither years nor time can erase the memory of Mother Herndon's dedicated service. It is my prayer that the spirit of evangelism will grip the hearts of our present-day evangelists to truly reach out for lost souls; taking seriously our Presiding Bishop's 2014 theme:

"We are Called to Minister and Witness
to a Deeply Distressed and Troubled World ."
(Acts 26:15-18).

Mother Herndon's memory will linger in the hearts of those who knew her. As the International Supervisor of Women for the Church of God in Christ, I pledge to promote her legacy throughout the church especially to the youth.

We cannot afford to forget the work, labor and sacrifice of this great woman of God. Through her work, Mother Herndon has increased the Kingdom of God.

Mother Willie Mae Rivers,
General Supervisor International
Department of Women, COGIC

Dr. Barbara McCoo Lewis
Assistant General Supervisor

FOREWORD

The historical archives of the Church of God in Christ would not be complete without documentation of the great exploits of Mother Reatha Herndon.

She, along with her twin sister, Leatha, will ever be remembered as true crusaders-who among others-blazed the trail for women in ministry. Their travels as evangelists included "praying out" churches across the country, many of which are still thriving.

For a short time, Mother Herndon served as one of the State Mothers of California. Mother Herndon was a profound teacher of God's word. She was tenacious in perpetuating the principles of Holiness and Sanctification.

She was a true soul-winner, who would never close her message without reaching out to the lost and hurting. Concerned about the youth's awareness of our rich heritage, she frequently cited historical reflections of our Founder, Bishop Charles Harrison Mason and the early days of the church. How blessed we were, here in Southern California, to be recipients of her love and strong faith.

Vivid memories linger of my visits to Mother Herndon's home as she freely shared her wisdom and experiences.

I commend Dr. Doris Sims, the author of this writing, for her selfless efforts to capture the succinct story of a true "General of the Faith."

Dr. Barbara McCoo Lewis,
Assistant General Supervisor
International Department of Women

Supervisor of Women
Southern California First Jurisdiction
Church of God in Christ, Inc.

ACKNOWLEDGEMENTS

It has been over ten years since I was called by Mother Herndon to come to her house to record her life's story. I considered this quite an honor.

She told me that she selected me because she believed that I would complete the project. She wanted her story to be told especially to the youth. Mother Herndon died in 2005 at 104 years old.

I thought that I had more time to put the book together since she told me that she was not going to die until she was 110 years old. I now had eight full tapes (weeks of interviews) and I was wondering how I should proceed.

I knew that Mother Herndon had entrusted me to get her book published. I was constantly mindful of her desire to have her life's story told- and what a story it is!

One day the way to approach the telling of Mother Herndon's story became clear. I was inspired to use Mother Herndon's own words; let her words speak for themselves. There was no need to retouch anything.

When I shared this with my Pastor, Elder Aaron Howard, he thought it was a great idea. He began to nudge me whenever it appeared that I had slowed down on the project. He would ask, "How is the book coming?" This would put a little more fire under me and keep me encouraged.

When Dr. Raynard Smith, Coordinator of COGIC Scholars, heard that I was writing this book, he would send word by Elder Howard to ask how the book was coming along. Occasionally, he would call and ask about the progress of the book and suggest a possible publisher.

When Mother Sue McCoo, who was the President of the Writers Guild for the Southern California Women's Department, First Jurisdiction, was told that I was doing this project, she encouraged me until it was completed. I thank her for her quiet support and inspiration.

Special thanks to Glenna Wilson, who was Mother Herndon's nurse for over thirty years. She heard that I was writing Mother Herndon's book and began to pray that this great pioneer's story would be distributed throughout the brotherhood. She also shared pictures from Mother Herndon's ministry.

Pinky Spann had in her possession the guitar and mandolin that were used by "The Twins" during their revivals. She brought them to my house for me to take pictures of these anointed instruments.

Doris J. Sims, Ph.D.
Author

ABOUT THE AUTHOR DORIS J. SIMS, Ph.D.

Doris Sims was born the third child of six siblings in Pasadena California a second generation native of California. She began her education in the Pasadena public schools where she excelled in creative expression.

Upon graduating from high school she enrolled in Los Angeles Community College where she majored in Home Economics. She then transferred to California State University at Los Angeles, to continue her major in Home Economics. Her desire was to become a home economics teacher. Upon graduating, Doris realized that her true passion was for teaching young children. She then pursued her

Elementary Teaching Credential. Her first teaching job was at Hooper Avenue Elementary School teaching first grade. While teaching at Hooper, she completed her Master's Degree in Elementary Education, and received a Reading Specialist Credential.

After a year, Doris decided to pursue her doctorate at Claremont Graduate University, majoring in Early Education or Child Development. She received a Fellowship to Claremont Graduate University. While studying at Claremont full time and working as an elementary school teacher full time, Doris realized that she needed to let something go. She therefore decided to quit teaching after four years and work part time as a college instructor. However, when she went to her Department Chair at Cal State LA to ask for a recommendation to graduate school, she was invited to teach in the same department that she graduated. This was the beginning of her teaching career at California State University at Los Angeles where she worked part and full time for the next 23 years obtaining the rank of Associate Professor. During those years she was honored as the Distinguished Alumni, designed Child Development courses for Head Start and early education teachers to be taught off campus courses through Continuing Education, was invited to be a guest lecturer in Taiwan, and conducted a study tour to China to research the one child policy and other cultural issues.

Upon graduating with her Ph.D., she founded and operated The Academy of Progressive Education, preschool through the 6th grade. After seven years she closed her schools and went back to Cal State LA. Later she founded two charter schools and a tutoring and educational consultant service.

For ten years Dr. Sims volunteered with the Chaplain's Eagles as a juvenile hall counselor providing Christian Counseling for the incarcerated youth and taught parenting classes to parents of incarcerated youth. She was also a Sunday School Teacher and became the Sunday School Superintendent for Chaplain's Eagles for all of the juvenile facilities.

She was a consultant for The Institute of Black Parenting and conducted monthly workshops to foster and adoptive parents.

Her experience in working with families and youth are vast and varied. Dr. Sims has written four children's books about African-American inventors with accompanying teacher's guides.

She conducts workshops for parents to churches, schools, and other agencies. She has presented at national and international conferences on child and family issues and has influenced the field of education and family relations for over forty years.

She has received numerous awards and commendations for her work in the field of child development and family relations. She is a consultant in all aspects of education and family relations. She is currently a charter school consultant where she assists community leaders, organizations and interested persons in developing charter schools.

Her passion is to assist in the education of the African American child and strengthening and restoring the black family.

Doris is an ardent church worker; her pastor is Elder Aaron Howard of Overcomers Church of God in Christ.

INTRODUCTION

Mother Reatha Herndon was one of the greatest women in Christendom. This was the conclusion that I came to from afar, long before I spent hours interviewing her. After that magnificent encounter, my conclusion was even more cemented. I had interviewed a woman that was over 100 years old. I have never been as impressed with anyone's memory as I was with Mother Herndon's. This woman of God could remember names, dates and places from over 70 years ago with complete accuracy. This gave real meaning to the scripture "...the Holy Ghost, whom the Father will send in my name, he shall teach you all things, and bring all things to your remembrance…" (John 14:26).

Mother Herndon, as she was relating her life's history, had total recall of events. I was convinced that this recording and the subsequent book about her life were God- inspired. Mother Herndon wanted her book to be a testimony of godliness and holiness to the youth. She wanted them to value education, realizing the degree of suffering it took to obtain the privilege. She wanted them to commit their lives to God at an early age-in their youth-as Ecclesiastes 12:1 admonishes.

Mother Herndon's entire life was a testimony of God's complete work in a person's life. Two young women, born identical twins, named Reatha and Leatha Morris, were destined by God to turn the world upside down. There were tremendous sacrifices for this feat to be accomplished. Their marriages failed; they gave up much comfort and security; they were criticized and talked about; Mother Herndon's children were raised by others. However, despite all of this, these two women planted 75 churches in the United States-many of which exist to this very day.

Truly, Reatha and Leatha were pioneers, spanning the horse and buggy age to the jet age.

These women of God lived through antagonism towards women in the ministry to an acceptance of their gifts and talents. Mother Herndon's mind was alert and active until her passing. She said that she was not happy because she had not accomplished her ultimate dream, which was to establish an Evangelist Training Center. At 104 years old Mother Herndon was still reaching for new heights and deeper depths in Christ. She was genuinely concerned about the education and training of those who would come after her.

After recording many hours of tapes, I was in a dilemma as to how to proceed. Then, the direction that I should take became evident. Let Mother speak for herself; do not paraphrase or change many of her words, and keep the information authentic. This is what I have endeavored to do. Mother Herndon's book was written by her. I just held the recorder and asked questions for clarification. These are her stories, her grammar, her intonations and vernacular.

Doris J. Sims Ph.D.
Author

CHAPTER ONE

The Beginning

I was born on October 11 in the year 1900, which was 35 years after slavery was abolished in 1865. I was born in Kingfisher, Oklahoma, to Reverend J.H. Morris and Sarah Morris. My father was born in Tennessee and my mother was born in Mississippi. They were forbidden to read or write. If they learned how to read or write, they would have been beaten severely. Therefore, they did not learn how to read or write. I was born in a region that was not a state; it was considered a territory. I had six brothers and five sisters. I was the eldest and twin to my sister, Leatha. I will talk about where I was born later.

THE MORRIS FAMILY

The twins, Leatha and Reatha are seated in the front row.

The real account of my life dates back to slavery. Number one, my mother and my father were both born slaves. My oldest brothers and sisters were born just at the close of slavery. Some of my brothers and sisters were old enough to be born in slavery, because my mother had 12 children that she gave birth to and for that cause, I date back to about 1900, which was 35 years after slavery had been abolished. The foregoing story of the end of the civil war is a true story of what was going on in my mother's and father's and my oldest brother's and sister's day.

Now, I want to say that slavery was a terrible thing. White folks ruled the minds of black folks. They had no rights and no privileges. Slavery took control of black folk's minds too. White folks said that black folks were not capable of taking care of themselves. It was common during slavery, when a young girl reached age 15 or older, that she could be bought by the "massah" and told that he now owned her and she must do as she was told. The young girls-against their will-had to submit to the sexual exploits of the "massah."

It was nothing but God that delivered the black people out of slavery because Abraham Lincoln said that if he could win the war without freeing the Negro, he would do it, but if he had to free the Negro in order to win the war, he'd do that. The war ended in Richmond, Virginia. What a great celebration took place! Because it was so far away, my mother and father were not in that celebration. They were not there, but they celebrated in the state and city where they were, which was Memphis, Tennessee.

Now, I want to say that during the Reconstruction days, the slaves were turned loose, without money, without homes, without anything. That's why I tell the young people today that they should give thanks to God. It was God who brought them out of slavery and took care of them. God gave them food to eat and an existence-to be able just to live. We wonder how they lived after slavery was over. We wonder how they lived. They were turned loose without anything. Yet, God made a way for the black people. That's why I say black people should always praise God and give God the glory for the way that He brought them out.

Now, my mother and father lived in Memphis, Tennessee during the end of slavery and the beginning of Reconstruction. There were two things that happened just as soon as the war was over. The white people had never known how to farm and take care of many of the labors on the farm-the black folks did that. Therefore, when the war was over the white folks had to find some sort of way to get along with the black people, because they didn't know how to do nothing much.

Therefore, they made an agreement with the black people. It's what you call "sharecropping."

Sharecropping means that the black folks would work for the old master or the owner of the plantation, for a part of the profit. The master or the owner would give blacks but so much, and he would keep so much for himself. Here's what happened: When a black man would go up to weigh the cotton to get his part of the money from the cotton, the white man would tell him a lie about how much money was in the cotton and how much money was coming back out of the cotton when it was sold and weeded.

When the Negro would ask the white man how much his part was worth and what came to him and the laborers, the white man told the Negro he had to go by his figures; he didn't have time to keep no books. The Negroes had to go by whatever the white man said his part of the sharecropping was and if he asked any questions it would cause a great calamity. Some Negroes were shot for asking questions about their part. Some were throwed in the river and some were abused much.

The Negroes found out that they weren't going to get no justice in sharecropping. They didn't have no such thing as justice. They had to take what the white man gave them and every year they would come out, deep in debt. They would owe so much after the cotton was picked and sold. They couldn't get out of debt and the white man wouldn't let them get out of debt. It looked like they were in almost the same fix as when they were in slavery. Then the black folks got together.

My father was with them when they got together down in the South. The first thing they did: they organized together. The black people did; the men organized. They sent out scouts throughout the entire South, to find out how black people were being treated after slavery. They found out from many people, that it wasn't no difference in the way they were treated during slavery and after the war was over. There were hundreds of black men in the South who came to the meeting.

They got together and formed a committee. The white folks asked them, "What do you call the committee?" The blacks replied, "We just call it 'the committee.'" The Negroes decided they were going to petition the government to gain justice for their crops and for fair treatment. When they went to the government to find out how much help they could get, they found out they couldn't get the help they needed to be able to survive. They decided that they had to do one thing and that was to get together as an organization and leave the South. That was the cause of my father and mother leaving the South. That sharecropping was just a joke. It wasn't nothing like no fair play. Sharecropping meant that the black man would get further and further in debt every year-not able to get out of debt.

The white people was still treating them like they did during slavery. Therefore, the Negroes decided to leave. When the black people of the South decided to leave, they left the South by the hundreds and then the thousands. They went everywhere.

Some of them went north to Kansas and around Ohio, up that way. Some of them went around Detroit and that way.

Some tried to go to Canada. Many of them had to stop at the line of Canada because they wasn't prepared to go into Canada. That is where the people came from that live right now in Minnesota-where my brother lived and died-because they couldn't go over the line into Canada, so they stopped trying to go. Many of them came over this way to Colorado, and as far as California and Texas. The reason for leaving the South was because of this condition-this sharecropping.

No help-nobody helped them or tried to protect them. The law wasn't for the blacks, and the law did not protect them and could not protect them.

They left the South by the thousands. This was called the Great Exodus or the migration of the blacks. Now at that same time, my mother and father were right there in it and there was a great rumor that there was land opened in the west.

THE SCRAMBLE FOR NEWLY OPENED LANDS IN OKLAHOMA 1901

It was many years after that, when we moved from what we call the east farm in Tennessee. This farm that we were moving away from was a place that the government had given to all that wanted a home in the new territory of Oklahoma.

The news had come to us that land was to be given away by the government in the territory of Oklahoma. That was how my father got on this land where the twins were born. That day when they got ready to leave (Tennessee) they had a raft made out of logs.

A typical river raft at the turn of the twentieth century constructed out of logs and ropes. NARA – ARC Identifier 516444

There were, I don't know how many people who got on that raft, with one horse and with all they brought, and all the things they wanted to bring, and floated across the Mississippi River. When they floated across the Mississippi River, when they had come to land, they landed in the territory of Oklahoma. There were two towns that I can remember.

One was named Guthrie, Oklahoma, which was noted to be the capital of the territory. Later on, Oklahoma City became the capital, the final capital, the real capital. My father settled there.

Anadarko Townsite, August 8, 1901. Auction in progress in lumber company booth. Temporary bank buildings & the beginnings of a lodging house nearby. NARA – ARC Identifier 516444

That morning, after the settlers came off of the raft from Tennessee, they unloaded all of their wares and got over to the place where the property was to be given away.

That morning they called all of those that wanted some property that came to claim property, to get in line. They all got in a long line, waiting for the cannon to shoot off.

When the cannon shot off everybody had to run, as far as they could run, or where they would run and stake down a flag. The flag that they staked down in the ground would become their home. That's what you call "settled it." There's

Anadarko Townsite, Oklahoma. Territory, August 8, 1901. A tent city in the cornfield – National Archives Records Administration – ARC Identifier 516446

another word too, that you call "stake down" or "staking down the settlement."

The government gave my father, and all those that ran that morning, 160 acres of land. My father staked down on 160 acres of land. My uncle, right next to him, got his 160 acres. I think one of my older brothers did too, but I don't remember that clear enough.

Anyway, that's where the twins were born, on that land that the government gave my father when he came from the exodus of Tennessee. Therefore, we had our home there.

We were born in the fall. There were hard

winters there in Oklahoma. Yet, the Lord took care of the twins. I wanted to make note of that in the book too-that God is able to provide no matter what happens. It was called a territory.

When they settled the United States there were various territories, such as Louisiana. I think it was ruled by the French. That's right-they was called Creole. The French came in here and got on some of the land in North America. The Dutch and various ones came from all over the world. The white man called this "a white man's country."

When they kidnapped the Negro and brought him from Africa over here, my father and my mother was in that. Their ancestors were in the midst of that. Everyone else that came over here could get recognition and get help, but the black man that emanated from Africa could not. Nobody helped him but God. So, they left the South by the thousands. My mother and father were among them that left the South. That's just before I was born. They left the South and they eventually settled in a place called the Territory of Oklahoma.

It was not a state. I was not born in a state. I was born in a territory. I was seven years old when Oklahoma became a state.

Now, here is one thing that so many of us do not

understand and know. That America-North America was full of Indians, thousands and thousands and thousands of Indians all over this country.

I was born in the territory of Oklahoma where the Indians were. They would come by with covered wagons. They would dig a ditch, buy a young cow, calf, and hog from my father, dig a hole in the ground and build a fire and roast them. The men-Indian men, did not wear britches. They wore skins around their legs. They wrapped the skins around their legs and that was their britches. On top of that, all of them wore blankets.

Ute Chief Sevara amd Family
Copyright, 1899. Detroit Photographic Company

I often wondered where they got the material to weave those beautiful blankets that they had. Anyway, the women were called "Squaws"-Indian Squaws. The men were called "Bucks."

Now, the men would have something on their heads. They would have something like a bonnet made with feathers, all kinds of feathers. I saw that when I was a little bitty girl.

I saw them with these feathers on their head. They had them "bonnets" so they would kinda come down on their back. The women would have blankets around them. That's the clothes that they

Praire Indians in Traditional Dress
http://lcweb2.loc.gov/service/pnp/cph/3c00000/3c01000/3c01200/3c01267v.jpg

wore. Women did not wear dresses, real dresses, dresses like we wear nowadays. They wore mostly blankets in those days. I often wondered about that. They traveled with wagons that had tops over them, like the top of an automobile but the top of those wagons was made out of canvas. It was made out of cloth. I wondered sometimes where they got that cloth from, but they got it.

That's the way that they roamed through the country. They didn't have no homes. Most all the Indians had was what they called "tepees" in those days.

Blackfoot Tipis on the plains
http://upload.wikimedia.org/wikipedia/commons/e/e9/Blackfoot_tipis.jpg

CHAPTER TWO

Growing Up

It was the year of 1900, October 11th. The weather had just begun to turn cold. On an early October morning my mother summoned my father to go get the midwife because she was in labor. When the midwife came to deliver the babies they did not know it was two of them and was surprised that there were twins instead of one.

It caused a great stir in the "new country" 'cause they had never had nothing like that. People came from far away to see the twins who they named Reatha and Leatha. My mother had to go to quite an expense of getting new clothes for both babies 'cause they wasn't expecting but one. It was quite a stir.

They always talked about that in my lifetime. People came from afar to see the twins in the new country.

One morning when we were about five years old, Mother sent the older children to look for Reatha and Leatha because we had gone missing. When they found us, we were at the side of the house that was made of sod. Papa had plowed up the ground and lay over the furrows and they hardened into bricks and had built the house out of sod.

One brick sod on top of the other 'til he got it up high enough to put a roof on it. He took the branches of the trees and made a roof on top of the sod house and dabbed it with clay; the ground was red clay in that part of Oklahoma. When it would get hard it would be like cement and it would not leak or give us any other trouble.

That morning, the twins was on the side of the sod house looking at a strange object. When they found the twins they asked them what was they doing. We told our sisters and brothers that we was looking at "it." "It" was a turtle, about as big as a wash pan. They were so scared when they saw that turtle looking at them, a live turtle coming out of that sod house, on the side where the sod was.

The turtle had its body half-way out, neck stuck out and looked at the twins, and the twins looked at it. We were too frightened to say or do anything. The turtle had got inside the sod.

Mama had the boys, my brothers, to go and pull that thing out of that rock, because for some reason Mama knew and Papa too, that that turtle was good to eat. So, that night we had some turtle soup. They told us about that all of our lives.

Another time we had a close shave, with what I suppose some would call death. We were out-my twin sister and I-in the yard, playing and we went so far from the house until they wondered where the twins was.

They put out a great search all around the house and down the way, kinda a little sketch of woods or brush to find the twins.

When they found them they were sitting playing with a rattlesnake. The rattlesnake was in a curl with its head stuck up from the curl. They were playing with the head of the rattlesnake and the rattlesnake was ducking his head from them and they were laughing about the rattlesnake moving its head every time they moved their hand.

We were just having a ball with our rattlesnake when they found us. It scared them so bad. They finally got us away from that rattlesnake without the snake biting us or doing any kind of injury to us, or those about us.

Another time, when we was real little babies-I suppose we must have been about three years old when this happened-we was out in the field with my father plowing. He had two horses or mules hooked up to the plow, and was plowing the sod, getting ready for the next planting that would be done in the new ground that had been broken up.

All at once-in that field-Papa happened to stop for a minute to see what was wrong with the animals because the mules or the horses that were pulling the plow had stopped. They were acting peculiar.

Papa looked down in the row where he had plowed and was plowing, and the twins was sitting down in the furrow playing when the mules, or the horses come charging toward them to carry the plow, and it scared my father so 'til he thought they was gone trample us down.

But they stepped right over us. God directed those animals so they lifted their legs high enough and stepped right over the twins and kept on going. Now those instances my father and mother and all my brothers and sisters told us about that all of our lives. So, I wanna thank God. God took care of the twins.

One Christmas, my mother or my brothers and sisters-somebody-had played Santa Claus. I still believe there is a spirit of Santa Claus-it's not no natural Santa Claus like they claim-the spirit of Santa Claus is the spirit of giving. That's what the word "Santa Claus" really means.

So we got up that morning, looked in our stockings, and there was a little book, along with some apples and oranges and candy stuff, for Christmas. That little book had pictures in it. The book was about the size of a post card, maybe a little bit bigger than a post card. That little book was made out of cloth. The pictures and everything, was printed on this cloth. We called it our cloth book.

My sister and I went back into the room and was talking to one another about this book. I said, "I tell you what let's do, Reatha." I called both of us by my name- we never did use but one name. I was Reatha and she was Reatha. They used to laugh about that. I didn't pay it no attention cause I didn't know I was doing that unconsciously. We called that our book. So we said, "We gon' go over here where Mama don't know and we gon' read to Mama what we found in our book."

My mother was born a slave and never did know how to read or write. She learned to read the Bible a little bit just before she died, and she was way up in her 70's. So we said to Mama, "we got to go to school, 'cause we got a book."

We was about four or five years old. Mama said, "You not quite old enough to go to school." We said, "Yes we are. We got our book. We supposed to go to school. We got our book."

Mama couldn't do nothing with us. We cried and carried on so, that she had to let us go to school with our older brothers and sisters. Sure enough, when we went to school, the teacher let us take in the class and recognized us with our cloth book and began to teach us how to read out of our cloth book.

Another thing that happened was when I was about 12 or 15 years old I had a demon enter into me. It would be called a fire demon. I had a demon in me that wanted to set stuff on fire. The first thing I set on fire-I remember it like it was yesterday-in those days we had bales of cotton.

Papa had just had the cotton baled, which was a very, very precious thing to farmers 'cause that was their income for the year that they was getting ready to take to the market. I was out there in the yard and got a hold of a cob, or a corncob. I cleaned that corncob off real good and made me a pipe.

I saw the old folks smoking pipes and I was gon' make me a pipe to smoke, too. I cleaned the cob out and made me a pipe. And I got me a match, and filled it (the pipe) full of somethin'- I don't know what it was; it must have been the leaves or something.

I filled that pipe full, and set that pipe on fire. When that pipe started burning, it set that whole bale of cotton on fire.

My mother ran out the house and saw that bales of cotton were on fire, and me sitting up there with it. It scared her so bad, 'cause that was four hundred or five hundred dollars going up in smoke.

Being immigrants, they could not afford it, having just come in to that territory. There, I had set their living on fire. Mama went in the house and got a blanket to put the fire out. She smothered the fire. I didn't know what I had done. It hurt my mother so bad she cried. It hurt me so bad to see her cry. I didn't know what the fire was all about, didn't know it was all that important.

The second time, I set fire twice. I was in the house, that we had just moved into not too long ago. This was after we moved away from the farm and we were living in a place called Enid, Oklahoma.

One day, that fire demon was on me, and I took a match and set the curtains on fire that were in the house that led from one room to the other. When Mama and my sisters came to see what happened, the whole house was on fire. They had a time putting that fire out.

As God would have it, it didn't do no real damage but it done damage enough. That was some of my real childhood. Now my sister, she never did do nothing like that. I was the one doing all the devilment.

Early one morning my mother received a telegram. My brother Tommy was in Kansas City, laying sick and could not get well. We found out later that he had cirrhosis of the liver. He told Mama in a letter that he wanted her to send for him because he wanted to come home.

So, Mother sent for my brother to come home. Sure enough, Tommy was sick and was there with Mama for quite a little while.

Two lodges in a Pawnee Indian village
Photograph by W. H. Jackson, 1871
www.gutenberg.org/files/37897/37897-h/37897-h.htm

PRAIRIE SOD HOUSES

When the pioneers moved to the prairies of the west, many were faced with a housing dilemma. There was a scarcity of trees and to import lumber was financially impossible. They saw some of the Native Americans, notably the Osage, Pawnee, and Hidatsa, making homes out of sod blocks and they adapted the method for their own use. Settlers were sometimes referred to as "sodbusters."

To build a sod house one needs grass that has densely packed roots. Buffalo grass, big and little blue stem, wiregrass, prairie cord grass, Indian grass, and wheat grass were ideal for this purpose. Originally, the process was to cut sod bricks using a spade, which was a difficult and laborious task. In the mid-1880s, a plow was invented that improved the process tremendously. It was called a "breaking" or "grasshopper" plow and cut the sod into strips one foot wide and 4 inches thick. A sod house required about an acre of sod.

Sod slabs were usually one foot wide and two or three feet long. The sod was usually laid with the grass side down. The bricks were placed alternately lengthwise and crosswise to increase the strength of the wall. Sod houses generally consisted of one room with divisions made by hanging blankets. If windows were desired, they were made of a wood frame with wood pegs driven into the sod wall. Roofs were made of thatch, or sod held up by poles.

African American Praire Homestead with a sod house
www.mrvanduyne.com/west/2013/Homesteaders2013.htm

Common materials used for roofs were poles of cedar or cottonwood, rafters of willow, cedar, or other wood, brush from wild plum and chokecherry, prairie grass atop the brush and sod over the prairie grass.

The "soddie" had some beneficial aspects. It provided excellent insulation so that it was easy to keep warm in the winter and cool in summer. Also, it served as an effective haven during those prairie wild fires. It was not unusual for the settlers to take in the cattle, horses, and pets during the threat of wild fires.

The negative aspects were perhaps obvious. The floor was usually dirt, the ceiling was constantly leaking muddy water during the torrential rains and snakes, mice, and bugs were everyday co-inhabitants. It was common for the woman of the house to have a canopy over the cook stove to prevent the above from falling into the stew.

CHAPTER THREE

Our Conversion

Before Tommy came, I want to tell you about the conversion of my twin sister, and I at 11 years old. We moved off of the 160 acres of land over to what we called the west home in Blain County, Oklahoma.

We didn't have no church out there, no church building. We were having services in just a little makeshift place. We had a pastor come out there and run a revival where we were in the country.

One day, while the revival was going on, my twin sister went out into the woods, which was right near the house. When she went out there, she stayed quite a while. When she came back, she came back shouting for joy, saying "glory" and "thank God." She said, "Oh Mama, I'm converted!"

She was only 11 years old but she said, "I'm converted. The Lord showed me that my feet had been placed in the Rock." Mama said to her, "No honey-not "in" the Rock, but "on "the Rock." Leatha said, "No, no Mama. He didn't say that. He said my feet was placed "in" the Rock. I stood there, looking at her, wondering what on earth had happened to my sister-my twin.

She kept on rejoicing and giving God the glory, and singing a little song, and all like that. Sho' enough, she was truly converted. She wanted me to get converted so bad, but I wasn't thinking about getting converted.

I was just old enough to start to thinkin' about doin' some devilment. The devilment that I would have started doing was learning how to play cards and tell lies, of course- and stuff like that. She kept on praying for me.

They had a baptizing and they baptized my twin sister. I saw her go in the water and be baptized. I wondered about that. I didn't like it too much but I let her go ahead, and didn't fuss at her about it.

Sho' enough inside of two more years, in a little town called Enid, Oklahoma, we had a Baptist church that my father belonged to and they had a preacher come there named "Westbrook." I will never forget him- Reverend Westbrook. He started the revival there in the church.

One night, in the revival he started a song about "It makes me sorry to think about Jesus, see how he died on Calvary, Calvary, Calvary." I was listening to him while he was singing that song and he was making a plea for us youngsters from school-that was there on the Mourner's Bench (a bench on which sinners prayed)-to come up.

About seven or eight of us was on the Altar. While they was singing that song, the girl that was sitting right by me-a school girl-with tears streaming down her cheek, she got up and gave the preacher her hand, which means she was converted. Right there on the Mourner's Bench, she was converted. When she was converted, it struck me like a bullet. She was sitting right beside me. I had been praying all day, saying "Lord, if you just convert me," 'cause I wanted to be converted like my sister was but I couldn't get no answer.

The last thing I remember telling God was, "Well God, I say if you don't convert me, I'm gon' to serve you, anyhow." That time, I turned loose.

Right there on the Mourner's Bench, beside my

"Revival Meeting" 1994 by Benny Andrews
http://www.turistaphotos.com/usa2001_full/template.htm

twin, and beside my little friend that had got up and gave the preacher her hand. Right beside them, when I said, "I'm gonna serve you anyhow," God struck me like an arrow coming from the bolt. God struck me and I went out like a light. I don't know what happened. I went out blank. I mean I went blank out.

They tell me I shouted all over the church-jumped up from that Mourner's Bench, and instead of going up and giving the preacher my hand, like the rest of them had done, they said I shouted all over that church. Not only was I shouting all over the church, my twin sister was out-shouting me.

Both of us was on the floor at the same time. I was giving God the glory because I had truly been converted. When I finally came to myself, I was sitting in the pulpit, with one of the church mothers standing over me, fanning me. I will never forget, as long as I live, Mother McPherson.

I looked up at her and wondered what on earth had happened to me. I thought, "Why am I sitting here on the pulpit?" Then the thought came to me, "You've been converted. You've been converted." Only twice in my life have I been out like that.

That's the first time in all of my life that I have been really unconscious. I mean just dead- don't know nothing. I was just 13 years old.

My sister had been saved two years. I was converted in 1913 and we went to church. It was on a Wednesday when they baptized me in water. Baptists have a way of having a baptizing like that, on Wednesday night, and then on another night they'll call the names of those that have been converted and baptized and ask them to lead out in prayer. So they had the prayer meeting in the Baptist church.

The pastor said, "Now Sister Reatha is gon' lead us in prayer." I was 13 years old. Lead us in prayer. My sister had prayed and then they called on me to pray. I started praying.

When I started, I was on my knees already-all of us were on our knees. When I started my praying in that Baptist church that Wednesday night, I went out again like a light.

I don't know what happened. Oh, thank you Jesus, that's why I know it's real. Yes, Lord. I went out like a light again! When I went out that time, like a light-thank you Lord- when I came to myself, people were laying on the floor all around me.

The church mother was lying in one place; the deacon was laying in another. All of them was lying around on the floor. What makes me remember it so well, is that I wondered as a child-at thirteen years old-what was they doing on the floor? They had been praying. They had been knocked out by the power of God. I know I been changed.

The angels in Heaven have changed my name. I, I know I've been changed. I, I know I've been changed. I, I know I've been changed. The angels in Heaven have changed my name.

We got around that big-bellied stove in the church because it was wintertime-it wasn't summer. While we were around that big-bellied stove, the power of God fell.

That's after we received the Holy Ghost. The power of God fell like rain. My brothers began to prophesy and give God the glory and praise and everything. The power of God fell on me. The Lord did two things for me that night. I prophesied about the war in Russia-*the war in Russia!* Exactly what the Lord showed me and gave me the prophecy about, the same year 1914, the war broke out.

When the Lord gave me that prophesy about Russia, around the same time, He made the whole Bible an open book to me and gave me the revelation and the interpretation of the scriptures. God gave me real revelation of the scriptures.

Now when I bring a message, when the Lord gives me a message, He gives it to me with great revelation to it.

This past Sunday, I brought a message. The name of it was, "It is Finished." "It" was the plan of salvation. It started here, and then it ends there. The revelation has to come in between, see?-of what happened and brought it to the finishing point.

I started out by telling about the three kinds of love: patriotic/friendship love, fidelity/mother's love and divine love. Now those three different kinds of love, the Lord gave me to speak about, in the interpretation, about what they really meant. For instance, I told them about patriotic love; how there was a man on the airplane that heard an announcement made by the captain of the airplane saying, "Somebody got to get off this plane. We are overloaded and if somebody don't get off we'll have a wreck. Somebody's got to give their life for their country." That was during the World War. He said that somebody got to get off the plane. That means that you've got to give your life for your country, because you're gonna get killed if you get off a running plane. Sho' enough a young man stepped forward and said he would gladly give his life for his country. Now that was patriotic love.

I told them how one man said to another, "I'll take your place if you don't get back on the date that you're supposed to be executed. I'll die in your place." I said *that's* friendship love. Jonathan and David had that kind of love, too. The Bible said the love was stronger than the love of women-*that* kind of love.

Then I spoke about the third kind of love-a mother's love. Then I spoke about the woman that stood and begged the unjust judge to save her son's life who was to go to the electric chair-that's what came out in the news some time ago. She pled with the judge to save her son's life because *that* was a mother's love. But I said there is a greater love; a greater love than any man has; that a man would lay down his life for his friend. Then I picked up Jesus, you know. The One who has the greater love, and then another scripture says, "For God so loved the world." I brought that scripture in, that "...Whosoever shall believe..." (John 3:16). Then I brought up how Jesus came in, stepping down through 42 generations, and was willing to give His life. "For God so loved the world that he gave his only begotten son that whosoever shall believe..."

Jesus gave His life for the world. Here is the revelation. Very few people have I ever heard mention this. In the ninth chapter of Hebrews, after Jesus rose from the dead, He went to heaven. What He went to Heaven for, was to report-this is revelations now-what He had accomplished on earth. He said that He was wounded for their transgressions, bruised for their iniquities and chastised. By His stripes we are healed (Is 53:5).

You know how the scripture goes like that. Jesus went through all of that because of what?-to give us a greater love, greater than patriotic love, greater than friendship love, and greater than a mother's love. That's that greater love.

Then He went to heaven and reported to His Father in that ninth chapter of Hebrews, that He went down to earth and accomplished what He had sent Him to do. Oh, it is wonderful. It just set my soul on fire. We were shouting from the pulpit to the door.

CHAPTER FOUR

Time To Be Educated

After we left the 160 acres that was given to my father by the government, we moved to a place in Blaine County, where there was a great big log house-a house made out of big logs and it was called a log house.

We left the 160 acres because there was a fraud that came up after my father had borrowed eight hundred. I'll never forget that eight hundred dollars. They defrauded him out of the 160 acres of land. He lost it because of that eight hundred dollars. He couldn't pay it. They took his land away because he couldn't pay.

Anyway, we moved to the west farm. It was full of blackjack trees, and the bark of those trees was good for medicine. My mother made tea out of it for everything that happened to us. She'd make us some blackjack tree tea.

Our schoolteacher lived in the house with us, because there was no schoolhouse where we lived. My father interceded to establish a school for his children, because we were out there in a bare territory. He sent for the schoolteacher to come. Her name was Myrtle Johnson. She had to stay in the house with us but the log house didn't have but one great big room.

There was about four beds in that big room. Mother curtained the big room off with curtains. I don't know where she got the material, but she curtained it off and made rooms out of curtains.

She gave the schoolteacher one end of that big room and curtained it off for her, and papa and the twins and her was in the other part. I think Myrtle Johnson was our teacher for at least two years.

When Myrtle Johnson left our house to go to the place that was built for her, we had to walk to school. Some mornings we'd get up, in order to get what little education we did get. Snow would be knee-deep everywhere-in some places, deeper than that.

But we had to go to school right through the snow, and wade through it-regardless of how deep it was-in order to get our education. The little house that they found or they built for the teacher to teach us in-the schoolhouse-was about one-half mile away, I suppose. We had to walk a long ways to go to school. The twins was about seven or eight years old.

We had to go through all of that coldness, bundled up with coats, 'muffs and everything.

Papa interceded when we got the teacher. The teacher was furnished to us by the government. I don't know what kind of arrangements was made concerning the government, but the government of the county-or something-paid the teacher, but the books came from the same place the teacher came from. What books we had.

I remember just as well, the teacher getting up in the morning telling us all to get up. She was the one who stopped us from eating breakfast. You couldn't eat breakfast and go to school because you'd be late.

Therefore, we learned to go to school without breakfast. When we came back we would eat. We went-my brothers, my younger brothers that were next to the twins and my nieces-to school, the only schooling that they got. They didn't get no further than about the fifth grade but me and my twin sister (by that time we was around 10 years old), my mother and my older brothers, all decided that we'd leave that farm and go to town.

The twins was born in the country, raised in the country, and didn't know nothing else but the country until then. When we went to town that was when we got a chance to finish our education. At town, Papa rented a house and we were in this particular house-the house that I set the fire to.

We went to school from that house. Now the schoolhouse was in Enid, Oklahoma, and the schoolhouse was a two-story house. Upstairs in this two-story house was for the higher grades. On the first floor of this schoolhouse was the first grade up to the eighth grade.

We had four rooms in that schoolhouse and we had four teachers. I can't remember all of their names. Professor Baxton was our teacher, and Professor Douglas was another one of the teachers. There were two more teachers, but I can't remember their names. By that time the twins were in about the sixth or seventh grade. We finished up to the eighth grade right there in that school.

The twins was so much alike. My twin sister and I favored each other so much that the teacher never did tell us apart. They called us Peter and Paul.

When the teacher would ask one of us to come to the blackboard to do the assignment, he would give us to work out the problem on the blackboard.

We were so near alike, until when the teacher would turn his back we would switch places. Leatha would take my place on the blackboard and I'd take her place.

I was smarter in arithmetic than she was, and she was smarter in history than I was. Therefore, I would take her place at the blackboard and work out her problem and when the teacher's back was turned, I would step back in my own place and work out my own problem. He never did know the difference.

We graduated out of that school in Enid, Oklahoma from the eighth grade and got our diplomas.

My mother and father had moved to Wichita, Kansas so we had to go to high school in Wichita. When we went to this segregated high school, there was only one high school in the whole city at that time. That was in the 1900's.

The whites were on one side of the room and the blacks were on the other, back in a corner somewhere. They curtained off, or put us in a certain corner-us black children-and had the white children one place in the same building, the same room, or in the rest of the room. I thought that was so silly.

We could hear the teacher teaching the information to the white children and then she would come to us and give us the same information. This was a lot of unnecessary work for the teacher.

Our books and other materials were old and raggedy. We did not have the same quality education as the white children.

Hattie McDaniel, who became a movie star later, was in that same class with me. If she was living today she could bear witness to what I'm fixin' to say. So Reatha and Leatha, we were twins, little black girls in this high school, we had started to go to in Wichita, Kansas.

All at once, we began to notice that my eyes began to give me a lot of trouble. My mother took me to the eye doctor and he was a white eye doctor.

We had to wait until all of the white people had been taken care of in the daytime, in his office and he would take me after the white folks had gone because segregation was knee-deep in those days.

While he was waiting on me and taking care of my eyes he finally told my mother and us what one of my troubles was-I had ulcers in my eyes. He took something like a toothpick and put some kind of medicine in the holes that were made in my eye with this ulcer and it hurt very badly but I endured and he closed my eyes up with a bandage until we come back the next day.

He worked on my eyes and thank God, that ulcer was healed. But my eyesight, the retina in my eyes had failed and was failing and because it was failing it got to the place I couldn't see a long ways off.

That was the reason why I had to stop going to school. I couldn't see the figures on the blackboard at all. So, I had to give up going to high school but thank God for what little high school education I got. I was there a little while, me and my twin sister, Leatha. We were both there for a little while.

CHAPTER FIVE

The Holy Ghost Fell

One morning, my mother received a letter from my brother, my fourth oldest brother. He was sick unto death and the doctors had given him up to die and said he couldn't get well. He was living in Kansas City at that time. He had got with a concubine wife and they had a little girl named Erma.

When my brother got so sick, he wrote Mama to send for him to come home. When he came home he was in the bed sick and it looked like he wasn't gon' get no better but my mother knew all about the herbs because she had a lot of Indian blood in her.

They were taught by the Indians to know how to mix different barks of trees. My mother would go out in the yard-when the children got sick or something-and pull up some weeds, bring them in the house, boil them down, make tea, and the children drank that tea and get well.

The Indians never did get ill. You know, Indians were here before America was settled by the United States. There were thousands and thousands of Indians here and they didn't have no drug stores and things. Just like the Indian, all of our medicine came from weeds and roots and barks of trees.

They didn't have all this sickness we have nowadays. So, my brother was laying there in the bed, sick. My oldest sister came in one day and said to Mama, "The Lord told me to have prayer for our brother that the Lord may undertake for him." Mama said, "Alright." I will never forget-it was on a Saturday. My sister called all of Mama's children together.

All of us was there in town except for two-Penny, my older sister, had died many miles away. My Mama had one more named Johnny, named after my father. He had been gone for years and I heard Mama-all my life-from the time I was old enough to hear and understand anything, talked about "My Johnny." "My Johnny's gone and I don't know where he is. I haven't heard from him, and I don't know whether he's dead or alive or what."

My twin sister and I got together and said when we got old enough we was gonna find Johnny and bring him back to Mama 'cause Mama worried about him so. Sho' nuff, we found him in his lifetime and brought him back to Mama-like I said-when we was old enough.

Anyway, he laid there, this fourth brother of mine named Tommy. He was sick unto death and my sister called all of us together to pray for Tommy's recovery or for the Lord to work some kind of way. She called all of us together in a room in this house, the same house I set a fire to.

My father was a Baptist preacher-you must remember-and she called him and all of us together. We all got on our knees to pray. My brothers was pipe smokers, cigarettes, drinking liquor, running women and everything else boys would do. They wasn't no Christians-weren't no real Christians.

They'd been converted but they'd wandered away from God but they were there-all of them were there. Papa chewed tobacco. He was a Baptist preacher but he didn't think it was wrong to chew tobacco. They all were there. My sisters-the older ones-dipped snuff. Mama was a regular snuff-dipper. She kept snuff. She had to have her snuff. She'd send that boy to get on that horse and send him a mile and a half down the road to the store, to get her a thing of snuff. That's the way we was, but we believed God.

We were Baptist and truly converted, some of us, some of them. The twins was converted but not filled with the Holy Ghost. All of Mama's living children was there but one. We got on our knees to pray. Lula-our sister that was next to us in birth-must have been about 20 some odd years old. My other sisters were all there and we got to praying.

We'd never heard nobody pray before in our life like Lula prayed. Lula got carried away in the spirit, while she was on her knees praying. When she got carried away in the spirit, she began to praise God. Her face was just wet with tears. Papa come running to her and said "Lula, baby." He saw her carried away and he didn't know what was happening to her. He started patting her, telling her, "That's enough now. Your Papa hears you and the Lord hears you."

Papa tried to console her, to stop her from praying like that but the more he tried to console her, the worst she got; the louder she got, and the more praying she did. As she began to praise God, she started reaching up and praising God; just praising God.

When she praised God, she just went off speaking in tongues and glorifying God. About that time, my other sister run out-the one next to her in age-and joined in with her. The Holy Ghost fell on her and she started to speak in tongues.

My brothers that was there in the house began to speak in tongues. The Holy Ghost came like the rushing of a mighty wind-just like it did on the day of Pentecost-and fell on them. It filled the whole house where we was sitting. The house got on fire for God!

Papa was running around, trying to see what was happening because he was a Baptist preacher and he was supposed to know the Bible and everything. Lula and them was just preaching it to him and glorifying God. About that time, Mama came in and seen all her children speaking in tongues, leaping, shouting and giving God the glory. She said, "Oh my God-all of my children have gone foolish!" Leatha and I were just shouting.

Our little coat tails was in the air! Mama said the Holy Ghost spoke to her and said, "They are not foolish." The Holy Ghost stopped her right there and said, "Remember Lot's wife." She didn't even know it was in the Bible 'cause she couldn't read. "Don't be like Lot's wife, doubting." She throwed up her hands-my Mama did-and said, "Oh God, if this is you, give it to me, too."

About that time, the Holy Ghost fell on her and she started speaking in tongues. Papa was still running around trying to see what was going on. My brothers went to him, cast the devil out-that's the first time we heard the word casting out devils-released them out of him, praised God and he started speaking in tongues.

They tells me we were hoopin, hollerin, shouting, going on and the whole neighborhood got on fire. They said somebody went out and called the fire department 'cause they said, "There's a ball of fire about the size of a washtub right over their house."

They said they thought the house was on fire. They thought the house was on fire! The fire department came and they said they found out that there was nothing but the Holy Ghost that had fallen there and the whole house was on fire. It was on Holy Ghost fire.

The Bible say it "appeared" to them like it was fire-it appeared, see. The tongue was like fire. My mother was speaking in tongues; my father was speaking in tongues and all my brothers was speaking in tongues. All of my sisters was speaking in tongues. One sister got up, ran in and said God raised her up and made her an interpreter.

I never knew no word like that was in the Bible-the word "interpret." One was speaking in tongues and the other was interpreting. We went on for one solid week. We went all night and all day. There was many times during that week, we'd sit down to eat and never did eat anything. We'd get up, go to shouting and giving God the glory. That's why I know it's real. The Holy Ghost is real. It's real. We had never heard about it; never heard a sermon preached about it; didn't know there was such a thing but the Holy Spirit just fell on us like it did on the day of Pentecost.

From then on we'd meet together-different times with my brothers and all that come over-but instead of sitting down and talking like ordinary people, we'd go to shouting and giving God glory.

For one solid week, we didn't eat, didn't sleep, and didn't do nothing hardly but just shout and give God glory.

My brother, he died one night. I woke up one night in that same room I said where the teacher had taught us. We only had one room, one room was by curtain. I heard something one night after that and my father had got out of the bed and was walking the floor. Was walking the floor, preaching, glorifying God, and praying. What woke me up was he was saying, "Oh, oh, oh." I woke up and said, "Papa, what's the matter Papa? What's the matter? What's the matter, Papa?"

He woke us up-me, my sister and my mother-that was in the room there. Papa said, "He just left. The angels just left. The angels was here to talk with me. The angel told me, 'I've taken your sacrifice and given you the Holy Ghost. I have taken your sacrifice and given you the Holy Ghost.'"

From then on, Papa never was worried about what that was because God told him it was the Holy Ghost. My brother that had died, God took him as a sacrifice and gave us the Holy Ghost.

There is another reason why I know the Holy

Ghost is real-as real as an experience a person can have. My brothers stopped drinking; they stopped chasing; they stopped all the things of the world.

My father stopped chewing tobacco. My mother stopped dipping snuff. All of that change come and nobody had told them nothing. Nobody told them, "Your dress is too short. You got to go home and change your dress." We didn't know nothing about that.

The Spirit that came in us, it made us willing to obey whatever the Lord said, regardless of our thoughts of what we wanted to do. I mean, we kept happy like that for one solid month.

Every time we'd meet together we'd end up shouting, speaking in tongues, prophesying and giving God glory. The police department came down-they say-to investigate what was going on and all around the house was filled with people.

The whole neighborhood was stirred with what was "going on in that house over there where the people were receiving the Holy Ghost." When they found out, they came down to arrest us because they said we'd all gone foolish. When they found out it was the Holy Ghost they got back in their cars and went on back to town.

Now all of that is the truth and nothing but

the truth. It's only one person left now to tell it, and that is me. Out of 12 children, they all dead and gone. My mother and father is dead and gone, so I'm the only one left of the 12 children that is left to tell the story. Thank God.

One day after that-I guess it was maybe a year after that-we came in and by that time, that was in 1915 that the Holy Ghost fell on 16 of us. There was 11 children and a sister-in-law, named Eleanor. There was another woman-that wasn't no kin to us-that was Mary Slaten, and then my niece, Ella. The Holy Ghost fell on her, too. With my mother and father, that's 16; 16 of us that the Holy Ghost fell on that night. We started in praying, like I told you she called us together to pray.

I guess it must have been about four o'clock in the afternoon on a Saturday. It was way up into the next day before we come to ourselves any kind of way. Every one of those died in the faith, we never backslid or nothing like that. That's right-died in the faith.

You know I had one brother; he was the most wayward one of mother's children. He died in the faith; he fell in line; he said the Lord chose him. We called him Buddy. We said Buddy was gonna fall in line, and he did before he died.

CHAPTER SIX

Making a Decision to Live Holy

One day my sister, my brother and I was lying crossways of the bed and we were talking among ourselves. What we were talking about was, "What are we going to do with this Holy Ghost that we have got. Are we gonna keep it, or are we gonna lay it down?"

We had a great discussion, because my brother at that time was 18 years old-just old enough to begin to like girls, and to go with girls-and the twins were about 14. Anyway, my brother and the twins, we lay across the bed and discussed it. I will never forget it because that made a great impact on my life, what we decided that day. What we decided among ourselves—just the three of us—was that we would rather die than to give up our Holy Ghost.

We made a concrete decision that, "This is it. We mean to keep the Holy Ghost, live or die; survive or perish. We gonna keep it 'til we die." Nothing would separate us from God.

That very day and from that very day 'til now-which has been over 75 years-I have lived holy. From that very day 'til now, I've never seen anything that I would even turn my head to leave God for.

God is better to me, as sweet to me and greater in my life than anything else. I love Him more than I do my own life. I'm willing to lay down my life any day for God. I've had a lot of temptations in my life, a lot of people pulling at me, doing this and doing that but I have never give over to no kind of temptations like that.

I've had all kinds of sexual advances at me, and even my sister have had 'em, too. When they would come after me with great sexual advances the Holy Ghost would stand up in me like a mule and it looked like the more they tried to advance, the bigger it got. I've never had no desire-none-to leave God for none of it.

So, I told them that whenever I get ready to go I want to be able to hear God say, "...Well done, thy good and faithful servant," (Matt 25:21) and I'm gonna bid this old world, farewell-that's it.

CHAPTER SEVEN

Protected By God

I remember how God protected me one day, from a band of white boys. One morning, as usual, the Lord would send me off to places to pray. I used to love to find a praying ground. I would go-I don't know where-to find a lonesome, right kind of spot where I felt I could meet God. I did that a lot of times in my lifetime.

On this particular morning I felt led to go to a particular place, and I can't tell you exactly where, but I went to a little swamp place, like down the hill. At the bottom of that hill, it was a level place there. Where that level place was, was where I was praying. All at once, I heard a noise and I said, "What in the world is that?" It stopped me from praying and everything.

It was a whole crowd-I don't know whether they were in a truck or in a car-of white boys. It looked like they were coming down there at me, to ravage me. They came at the top of that hill-I will never forget that-and started hollering at me down there.

I was about 50 feet from them and the Lord told me to run. So, I got up from there and ran. I ran up on the other side from where they were. They couldn't get to me unless they went and turned around or something like that. I went up this hill and that way, I got up quicker than they did.

A gang of them had decided they was gonna get the *little black girl* but thanks be to God, He protected me.

CHAPTER EIGHT

A Commitment Made to God

Now at this time, we were about the age of courtship. We-the twins-were in our teens, just entering into our teens. My brother, who was just four years older than us, we all were entering into that age. Because of that age, I began to have a lot of temptations.

There was a beautiful young man that was in our neighborhood at that time. It seems as though he fell in love with me and I suppose I fell in love with him. One day, we was sitting in a certain place and talking, and he said to me, "Reatha, let's run away and get married."

I told him that I wasn't prepared to do that-I didn't want to get married right now because I had some work to do for the Lord and I just couldn't afford to do that.

My sister was right along with me on those same ideas. There was a young man who wanted to marry her but it was right at the time that the draft was being made for the soldiers for the First World War.

This young man wanted to marry my sister before he went to the army; before he was drafted into the army. We had just got together and made our commitment to the Lord that we would not let nothing separate us from God and from our Holy Ghost.

These young men were not saved and they didn't have salvation. They didn't know nothing about that. So, this young man did go on to the First World War in 1914 or '15. By that time, Reatha and Leatha were of the age that we had to make a decision whether we were gonna give our life completely to the Lord or whether we were gonna get married and get tangled up with a lot of sex activities.

We decided that we would die before we would go off and let them take us into a lot of sex activities and take us away from God. For that cause, we leaned away from all of that and began to give ourselves to God, insomuch until we begin to work in a revival.

My brother put on a real revival about that time and was preaching out a church, a Pentecostal church. Reatha and Leatha got with him and begin to help to preach out this church. I did everything in the church: Sunday School, president of the Sunday School, Superintendent and everything else in the church to help begin this church.

The last thing we did in getting this church going was, we put up a tent. My brother put up a big tent, right there in Wichita, Kansas. When we put up this tent that was the first time in my life I'd ever seen anything like that.

I don't know how he learned how to do it, but he did. He was way yonder older than us. In that tent many people got saved and was blessed of God. At that time, we were about 18 years old when we put that tent up but many people were saved and blessed in that tent. Now, in that tent was where I brought my first message.

Now, I told you about one night how they came and woke us up late at night and told us, "Get up quickly and come downstairs 'cause Papa is leaving us tonight. I went downstairs around the big, pot-bellied stove- that would burn wood and coal in the wintertime-it was called a heater. Around that stove, that night, the power of God fell on us as usual. Whenever we spent our time together, we spent most of our time shouting, giving God the glory, speaking with tongues, interpreting tongues and getting messages from God.

That's what the time would go for when all of the family got together, after the Holy Ghost had fell. So this particular night, when Papa was gonna leave us, he was going to die. The power of God fell that night and all at once the Holy Ghost came to me—Reath—when I was about 17 years old.

The Power of God came over me that night and the Spirit of God anointed me with the gift of wisdom. That night, Papa died.

CHAPTER NINE

From Baptist to Church of God in Christ

Now what happened, it was the night the Holy Ghost fell on us. It was 16 of us that the Holy Ghost fell on that Saturday night, the 26th night of June, 1915. After that, the Holy Ghost started to working with all of us; speaking with tongues and glorifying God.

We went forth to minister and carry on in the Holy Ghost way until the Baptist folks put my father out of the church because they didn't believe that speaking in tongues and the Holy Ghost was real. They thought it was a cult coming forth.

When we was indulging in that, for that 'cause they didn't want to get that mixed up in the Baptist church. For that cause, my father had to go ahead and work in the Holy Ghost way, instead of going on with this Baptist way. So, that was the thing that separated us from the Baptist church-it was the Baptism of the Holy Ghost and speaking in other tongues, as the Spirit give utterance.

They didn't believe in it. It was years after that when the Baptists began to read the Bible, especially that eighth chapter of the Acts of the Apostles, where Paul went down to Samaria and preached.

Many people was baptized in water and they sent for the Apostles to come down to Samaria to lay hands on them and the Bible said they received the Holy Ghost-these converted folks.

I've had people say to us, "Don't pray for me. Don't put your hands on me 'cause I got the Holy Ghost when I was converted," but that is not so.

The Bible says that they had been converted and baptized in water but they did not have the Baptism of the Holy Ghost. The Apostles laid hands on them, those converted folks; those folks that was baptized in water.

I say sometimes in explaining it, that they was already members of the Baptist church but they needed the Baptism of the Holy Ghost. So, they laid hands on them and they received the Baptism of the Holy Ghost. Also, in the 10th Chapter of Acts it says they received the Baptism of the Holy Ghost and speaking with other tongues as the Spirit gave utterance. That separated them from the Baptists.

Down through the annals of time, the Baptists began to read the Bible and found out that the Baptism of the Holy Ghost is all through the Acts of the Apostles, and some of them have received it. Now they do not fight it like they did in those days.

Now, after my father and brothers was put out of the Baptist church they established their own church. That is why Bishop Mason walked out of the Baptist church and established the Church of God in Christ. After they established their own church, my father had started preaching out churches and many people were saved before we knew anything about the Church of God in Christ. What happened to us after the Holy Ghost fell on us the 26th night of June, 1915 was my brothers started their own Pentecostal church. They didn't know nothing about the Church of God in Christ. They'd never heard of it. When O.T. Jones came to our house in Wichita, Kansas and explained to us about the Holy Ghost, about the Church of God in

Christ and about Bishop Mason, my twin sister and I went to Memphis and found out there were a lot of people there that were filled with the Holy Ghost like we were; speaking in tongues like we were and we didn't even know nobody in the world had it but us.

When we found out all these other folks had something just like we did, we were so happy. That's how we joined in with the Church of God in Christ. When we joined in with them, Mother Lizzie Robinson gave me and my twin sister a letter of recommendation to go unto all the world and help preach out and establish churches that are speaking in tongues as the Spirit give utterance-that's called a Pentecostal church.

My father never did just come over to the Church of God in Christ, 'cause he didn't know nothing about it but he was filled with the Holy Ghost and was with my brothers in a Pentecostal way. They never did just get with the Church of God in Christ in a way of speaking because they didn't know nothing about it. They were just trying to build up among themselves but Reatha and Leatha, especially me-from the time that Mother Robinson gave us these letters of recommendation-I was with the Church of God in Christ.

I never did work with my brothers like I could have done. The reason why I did not work with them is because they didn't have the outreach and the places that I could go and minister, labor and tarry with people.

Other folks-in other words-the larger congregations, had a larger crowd of people to work in and to work among, so I stayed among them at Church of God in Christ.

CHAPTER TEN

The Beginning of My Ministry

A book opened to me, and all of the Bible became like a living book to me. I was given the gift of wisdom to understand the Bible. I understood what it meant when we read it; what it said. The hard words that were in there-the Lord give me how to pronounce them, how to analyze them, and how to get the interpretation of hard Bible sayings in the Word. Such as this, I said to Mama that night-that very night, I remember it like it was yesterday-"Oh Mama.

The whole Bible has come open to me and I understand everything that is written in there." She looked at me in great surprise. I said, "Ask me any question that you want to ask me about the Bible and I'll answer you." They started shooting questions to me. One of the questions that they sent to me (I forget who it was that directed it to me) was, "Alright Reatha, since you know everything, got everything together there- how can a man live free from sin?"

I said, "Oh, here's the way that's done. When a bucket is filled with water you can't put nothing else in it. If you keep water running in it, because it's steady running down the bucket, it will run over, full of water. That's how it works. We don't let sin rest in our heart, in our body and in our mind.

We let it flow off like the water would flow off from a bucket full of water." All of them marveled about that-how sin would come alright and present itself to us but we wouldn't let it enter in. So the Bible says, "Let not sin therefore reign,"-which means rule us you know-"in your mortal body" (Rom 6:12).

God opened all of the dark sayings, which are opened today. Today the dark sayings of the Bible are opened to me 'cause the Bible is full of dark sayings. One time the disciples asked Jesus why He spoke in dark parables that were all black to them. Jesus told them that it's not for the children of the world to know the interpretations of these things, but it is revealed to them that are born again-that's what in substance He says. So, with that cause I went on from there.

Now the first message that I brought, was from the fifth chapter of Galatians and the 25th verse. Here is what it says, "If we live in the Spirit, let us also walk in the Spirit." Now as a child that's 18 years old, that didn't know nothing about no Bible-'cause I'd never studied nothing like that in my life-this was revealed to me. I said, "What it means by 'living in the Spirit, walking in the Spirit,' is day by day, accomplishing what the Bible tells you to do-do it. That way, by you doing what He tells you to do day after day, that is walking in the Spirit."

The Lord give me to understand the real things. From then on, my brother would give us the chance to testify in this tent. This was the beginning of my ministry.

Now my twin sister did not start in the ministry right when I did. I got the anointing first, and then she got the anointing later. In this tent meeting my brother would let us get up and testify, and when we would testify the Lord would start to give me messages-various messages the Lord would give me and I'd begin to quote scriptures. You know when you testify, you're not supposed to bring no message, but you're supposed to tell what God is to you.

But soon I would begin to tell the various messages that the Lord gave me. One of them was, "Living Free from Sin. Another was, "How to Walk in the Spirit" and all those kind of things. I begin to get the revelation of different Bible verses and quotations and to give them in what would have been a testimonial and see what the Spirit was gonna bring forth. So for that cause, that's how I got started. Every time I got up to speak, the Lord would reveal and unravel some kind of scripture to me.

My twin sister-instead of going forth like I did-she'd get up and start and then say, "Well Reatha, what did it say?" about so, and so. I had to tell her what to say. That went on for quite a few years. Even when we started traveling, I had to tell her a lot of times what to say. Finally, she got the real anointing and brought forth great messages from the Bible. Now, the next revival was the beginning of my ministry. The next time there was a town in the state of Kansas, named Hutchinson. Hutchinson was about maybe 200 miles or so from Wichita, Kansas. It was in the west part of the state of Kansas.

There was no church-not in one city in Kansas. They didn't know nothing about the Holy Ghost-never seen nobody with it, never heard about it.

CHAPTER ELEVEN

Introduction to the Church of God in Christ

In the year of 1919 the twins went to what would have been called the first "Convocation" I suppose we call it a Convocation now, but it was just getting together as a Convocation in Memphis, Tennessee.

Just before we went to Memphis, while we had that tent up in Wichita, Kansas in 1918, one day a little old man came to our house. We didn't know who he was, never saw him or heard of him in my life. He came on in and talked with my mother and father and got us acquainted with him and all, and it turned out to be O.T. Jones, Sr.

He met my mother and father and we bought a watermelon. I will never forget that day he was there, we bought a great big watermelon and cut it and we all was eating watermelon on the front porch with O.T. Jones.

While he was there talking to my mother and father, he said "I've got a revival that's gonna be in Newwater, Oklahoma and I want you to let the girls (we was 18 years old at that time) come down and let them be with us in this revival. Mama didn't believe in letting us leave home much, but for some reason she was willing to do it. She let Reatha and Leatha get with O.T. Jones, Sr. and go down to Newwater, Oklahoma.

That was my first missionary trip from home. When we went down there in Oklahoma is the first time in my life that I saw people tarry for the Holy Ghost, 'cause we didn't tarry for Him-the Holy Ghost fell on us you know? I saw them saying, "Jesus, Jesus, Jesus, Jesus." Then I said, "Is that the way to tarry-I wonder-for the Holy Ghost?"

That's what I saw them doing, and every once in a while somebody would get "it." O.T. Jones, Sr. told us about Bishop Mason, the Church of God in Christ, and about how they had churches

Leatha Reatha

everywhere. It was a large organization, 'cause we'd just started you know?

He told us he wanted us to come to Memphis, Tennessee in November, when the meeting would be. We promised him, by the help of the Lord, that we would go to the Convocation in 1919. Sho' nuff, when 1919 came, Reatha and Leatha got on the Jim Crow car-the Jim Crow train, and we rode down to Tennessee and got to the meeting called the Convocation.

Now, that's the first time I ever saw Bishop Mason-a little black man. He wasn't nothing to look at. He was very, very homely, but filled with the Spirit. He was there, singing with his sweet potatoes, talking about God made the sweet potato. The sweet potato was looking like a man's head sometime.

Bishop Mason would have a stick, and it would be crooked, and he said, "This is a crooked stick, like the snake," and he'd preach on that. He preached about sweet potatoes, sticks and all kinds of vegetables and things.

One time, a lady came to the Convocation and brought an egg, during the First World War. On that egg, it was handwriting on the eggshell. The writing that was on the egg said, "Millions at war," on that eggshell. He carried that eggshell with him all over the country, preaching about the wonders of God. There were many, many things he preached about with those sticks, potatoes and all. If they resembled anything, he'd take a text and preach off of it, maybe for two or three months.

CHAPTER TWELVE

Receiving Papers to Evangelize

In that meeting of 1919, Mother Lizzie Robinson-who was the Head of the Women of the Church of God in Christ-said to Reatha and Leatha-the twins-"I want you girls to work with us in the Church of God in Christ and help preach out churches.

The preachers are preaching out churches everywhere and you can help them and travel all over the country and preach out churches." We were listening at her talk like that. Now, they wasn't giving nobody no licenses in those days but she said, "I will give you a letter of recommendation to the preachers and wherever you go, you'll show this letter to the preachers that are trying to preach out a church and he'll let you all work along with him."

"The Twins" were so anointed by God Himself, until the fear of God was upon the preachers and they were afraid to bother or stop us. Bishop Mason said, "Let the girls alone." One day I was standing at the pulpit, and Bishop Mason started reaching for me to come to him. When I turned around and went over to him, he put me on my knees between his knees, laid hands on my head and prayed for me. If I had been a man it would've been said that he ordained me.

When I got up, he told me "to go into the "everywhere" and carry the gospel. Ever since that day, I have been carrying on. Live or die, sink or swim,-enduring whatever persecution that would come upon me. Through our ministry, God has been with us all of the way.

That was the beginning of us going forth in the evangelistic work. We helped to preach out these churches. When we first started, we didn't go among these churches expecting to give no message-that wasn't it.

The people would call it preaching-we were not that. What we did was work around the altar. We'd get people around the altar-15 or 20-sometime on a long bench, called a Mourner's Bench.

We'd put them people on that Mourner's Bench and then we'd get over those people, casting out devils, praying for them and blessing them. Every once in a while, somebody would jump up and just shout for joy that had got completely delivered. We would let them help us pray for the others. That's how we got started. Sometimes in the meeting there would be 15 or 20 people who would get saved. Most of them would be filled with the Holy Ghost. That's how we would help preach out, and pray out those 75 churches in the Church of God in Christ.

Many places we went never heard of no Holy Ghost before, never heard nothing about it. The people didn't know about the Holy Ghost. I remember one place that we were in one time, we went to this place down in Missouri. The people didn't know nothing about the Holy Ghost. So, we were carrying on this particular service down there.

We had 19 cents between us on Christmas Day; didn't have no Christmas dinner like what we'd been used to at home, you know- apples, oranges, nothing like that. We were singing that song by John Wesley Work III, "Lord, I'm Out Here on Your Word." We was telling God that we was out there trusting in Him. About that time, we were holding this service in this church building where the people were at the altar getting saved and blessed. All at once, a great influx of white people came in the front door-about 35 or 40 of them I guess altogether, young people.

Where they'd come from was from downtown. All the stores closed because "the girls" were in town-10 cents stores, Kress stores, Woolworth stores. It was a little town, anyway.

All the stores closed up and the white folks come to the meeting. It looked like the young people were there to make fun and laugh about what we was saying, and doing, speaking in tongues like that.

So they all stayed there in this place while we carried on this meeting. Before they left, they strung in a line and passed by the table and left enough money for us to buy ourselves tickets the next day out of town. God just sent them there in time to get us the money for our fare. I will never forget that. It is a church in that place today. That was one of those 75 churches.

CHAPTER THIRTEEN

Revivals Across the Nation

Reatha and Leatha and Samuel Crouch was at church. Now, I want to talk about the first revival that Reatha and Leatha indulged in, in this country. Reatha and Leatha's revival was the first time that anybody was able to bring forth any kind of result with the Pentecostal gospel in San Francisco.

The very first church got together to have a street meeting. There were very few buildings that we had any kind of service in. We had a whole lot of our services on the street. This time we got together to go on the street, and I don't know where Leatha got it from, but she got some red bandanas-a red rag anyway, and put them around her shoulder.

I don't remember how it got on my shoulder. She went out on the street with this red rag around her shoulder and I think she had her tambourine. I had something. I used to strum a guitar, you know? I used to play a guitar on the street.

Anyway, we went out on the street and the people come running from every which way to see what in the world this new thing that was going on. Together, we'd sing like that and play our music like that until the people gathered. When they gathered, we would start a message talking about the Baptism of the Holy Ghost. "For the promise is unto you, and to your children, and to all that are afar off, even as many as the Lord our God shall call," (Acts 2:39).

Sometimes the Lord would break them down, they'd be crying in the streets. I don't remember them kneeling particularly in the streets, but they did shout and worship God. Anyway, they got really blessed of God in the street.

What we did in San Francisco-I remember this clearly- they came into the building. We had invited about 50 or 100 of them in front of the church, out on the street there. We told them,

"We want all of you to come and go with us in the building." We'd fill up this building when they'd come in, we'd fill up all the seats. Then we would have "tarry service." We would sing Marvin V. Frey's, "Come by here good Lord, come by here." After a while, the power of God started raining down. People started falling out, gettin' filled with the Holy Ghost, gettin' born again and being blessed of God.

When we left there, we'd leave a church. We'd leave so many people until they needed a pastor.

The church organization would send us a pastor. We'd leave a pastor there over them, and that was how a church was established.

I will never forget when I was in St. Paul, Minnesota. Now remember, that's been 50 something years ago. We were there-Leatha and I-on the 4th of July, and we were in a little tent. It was a small tent this preacher had put up, and he had the twins there, carrying on this revival. I will never forget them throwing fire crackers in the tent, on the 4th of July, while we were carrying on and talking about the Baptism.

Some of the youngsters in the neighborhood gathered around the building. In those days, we just had a little storefront building. The only way we had any service at all-we had no real churches-is that we would rent these storefronts and they would let us have service in there. In this little storefront building we had a little tent. You put a little tent outside of the building-right by the door of the building-that would keep maybe around 100 people in those days.

Those young people started throwing firecrackers in our meeting, into the tent. They tried to run us away from there and tried to break up our meeting. So, we prayed to the Lord, rebuked that devil and God went on and saved the people in a mighty way in that meeting. That was the beginning of the Church of God in Christ in St. Paul, Minnesota.

There was another time we was in Texas, and that was about 1924, with Bishop Crouch. We were in Fort Worth, Texas with a pastor named Love. He had a church and had us come to his church for a revival. In those days of Reatha and Leatha-by me strumming the guitar and she played the mandolin-there wasn't a building that held the people. Every building was jammed and packed.

In some of the places, all of the doors was packed, all around the walls they was packed.

NATIONAL EVANGELISTS

"And he gave some, apostles; and some, prophets; and some Evangelists; and some, pastors, and some teachers; the perfecting of the saints, for the work of the ministry, for the edifying of the body of Christ."

ROLL of HONOR

Arizona Drain
Hattie Fray
J. C. Fitzpatrick
N. Anderson
Bertha Richardson
Nellie Briggs
Estella Donaldson
Hattie Crockett
Allie Steele Crutcher
Ruth Goodwin
Magnolia Woodward
Pauline Coffey
Leatha Chatman
Maggie Cleveland
Rosetta Young
Mother Jordan
Emma Woodward
Susie McDaniels
Maggie Matthews
Susan Cook
Leon Mainor
Leslie Smiths
Cora Berry
Leina Cunnigham
S. C. Mainor
Mary Crawford

MRS. REATHA HERNDON
Los Angeles, California - Chairman of Women's National Evangelistic Board

LEADERSHIP CONFERENCE

In the Leadership Conference, there are no titled Officers. (Leadership Conference.)

One man said he hoped he don't see that many people at his church no more, too many people. We carried crowds like Katherine Kuhlman. We carried those kinds of crowds in our day. There are some few people living today that know about that but most of them are dead and gone.

In New York, the Jews and the Catholics swore that they wouldn't rent no building to the holiness ministers to hold meetings. They wouldn't rent or make no room for them, no kind of way. They were real hard against them but Mother Payton went in there and some kind of way stood up against them.

You know, the Lord give women the courage to stand up to them. Mother Payton went in there, some kind of way she found her way there and staked down a little Church of God in Christ.

When she got it staked down well enough to send Bishop Mason word that she had this little place, she sent for him. I'm telling you that we ought to stop talking about women preaching so much. Everyone should go on and do a work for the Lord. Let the people say what they want to. When Mother Payton got the church started good, she sent for Bishop Mason to send somebody up there to really help get the place established.

Sho' nuff, eventually some of the preachers used to go up there but they're dead now. Every one of them that I knew died-the one that they called the little dancing preacher. Thompson, he went up in there, among the old ones that I know about. Anyway, she opened the way, cracked it open you know. Then Kelly, you know him-O. M. Kelly? He just died not long ago in New York. He went up there.

He was the first one that built a church because they wouldn't even sell him no ground! They was against the Holiness up there. Bishop Kelly was the one that really opened up the thing-wide open-so that "Whosoever cometh let him come," but Mother Payton was the first to start a little church in New York.

CHAPTER FOURTEEN

Evangelizing the 75 Churches

Me and my sister Leatha-known as the "Evangelist"-called ourselves "the little twin sisters" 'cause we was young at that time, and skinny too, little in stature. We traveled all over this United States, from New York City-the northern part of the United States-all the way to the southern part.

For instance, the first church that was ever in San Francisco, Reatha and Leatha went with Bishop Crouch in those days and we were helpful in establishing the Church of God in Christ there. Way back there in those days, "Holiness" was not known all over the United States, as it was now known as a real Pentecostal, baptized with the Holy Ghost and fire organization. We were just breaking through in many places.

The next place I can remember we had a wonderful service was in Buffalo, New York at 501 Clinton Street. I will never forget that number. We went there and the Lord blessed it in a mighty way. There were some young people that had just got saved-especially young preachers-and they were there. We were young in those days and I was single. All of us got together and we would have a meeting there in that building-at 501 Clinton Street-shouting, dancing and praising God. One of the things I thank God for is that in those days we had the altar-the Mourner's Bench.

We'd get people on the altar and pray with them and sometime it would be way up in the night, and we'd stay with them until God brought them through. God would bring them through shouting, dancing and giving God the glory.

We all would have a great shouting account. Every time one came through, we'd get them up off their knees and get them started working with the others-that's how the meeting was. When one would get through and receive the Holy Ghost and be wonderfully blessed of God, we'd get him started working with others. Sometimes it would be 15 or 20 people getting the Holy Ghost, getting blessed in one night.

That's how we helped to build and pray out these churches. When we left these places, we'd always leave a lovely crowd that had been saved and really blessed of God. Many of them were filled with the Holy Ghost and we left a pastor there with them to carry on. That was the beginning of the Church of God in Christ. That was in Buffalo, New York. That's one of the places the Lord gave us a great big church.

Then we moved from Buffalo to New York City. There wasn't no church in none of these cities. We were praying out churches and getting them started. So, in New York City, that's where the Lord blessed in a great way. We didn't have no church there, just a storefront building and one or two preachers had been there a time or so before we got there.

It looked like they couldn't get the church going or something. Finally, we went there and the first time we went there it was with a man called Metcalf. Metcalf rented a place over a garage that seated about 200 people.

One of the girls was anointed to play the piano. Metcalf would get her started playing that piano early in the evening and she'd play it at least an hour before service, while the people are gathering. That was the beginning of that revival. We were there at that particular revival at least 30 days or more. Many people were saved and filled with the Holy Ghost. In those days, God did a lot of healing. People were healed in those days, of all kinds of diseases.

Me and my sister laid hands on people and God blessed the people to be really delivered through the laying on of hands, and God healing them and then God would save them. A lot of young men that are preaching the gospel today was saved in those meetings.

Therefore, all of those churches, in the beginning of their ministries and beginning of those churches-all over the edge of the United States, between the United States and Canada-we helped preach out, dig out and pray out those churches, in San Francisco, California, St. Paul, Minnesota, Buffalo New York, and New York City. Those churches are standing and prosperous today because of our ministry.

Many years after that we would go back and forth. As time went on, the Lord blessed me to learn how to play the guitar and my sister to play the mandolin,

Guitar (above) and Mandolin (belw) that Reatha and Leatha played when they evangelized

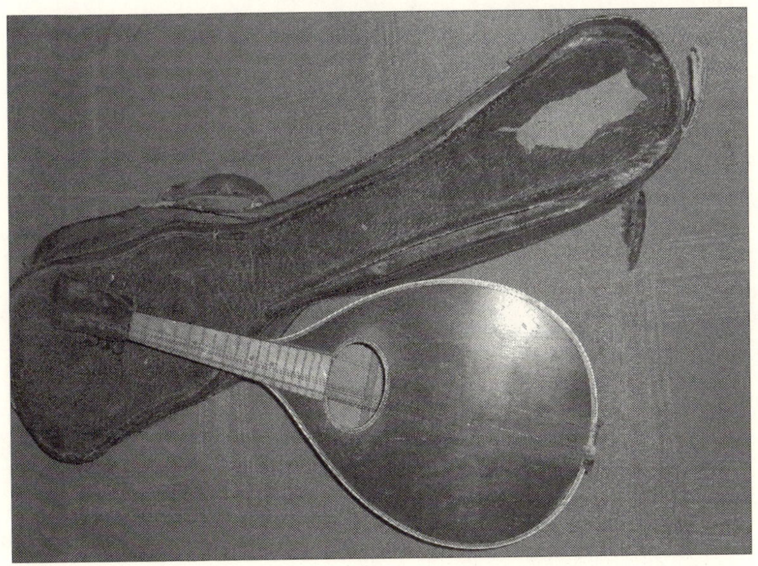

so we had music along with our singing. We'd sing a song like the one by Alphus LeFevre, "I'm gone to take a trip in that old Gospel ship and go sailing through the air. I'm gonna shout and sing until the heavens ring and I'll bid this old world goodbye."

We'd sing those songs and the whole church-the whole audience-would go up into shouts. In those days, there would be all the way up to 15 or 20 people who would get saved in those revivals.

That was the beginning of many of those churches, through that part of the country.

From there, I remember another great revival that we carried on in St. Louis, Missouri in 1919. We had a preacher there named Elder Bostick. We didn't have no bishops in those days-everybody was an overseer or an elder.

So, we had this church there in St. Louis, Missouri, where in the week time they'd meet downstairs and on Sunday they'd meet upstairs. While the twins were there, all the places-upstairs downstairs-was full. The pastor said he'd never seen that many people in church before in his life. The whole church was full. The people was jam-packed.

That was the first place that I remember seeing the Lord just doing all kind of miracles. In that meeting, I remember God healing people of tumors, cancers and all kind of sickness and conditions. One woman had a goiter on her neck. The goiter was so big on her neck, it just filled the whole side of her neck. It stood up from her ear and came straight down. We laid hands on it, in the name of the Lord and God completely healed that woman and removed that goiter!

Many people was healed of tumors and things. Women had tumors in the stomach-God healed that. Many people were healed and delivered. God set that whole city on fire. It was one of the greatest revivals ever run in St. Louis.

Many people were saved. We helped establish that church with Elder D. Bostick and his wife, Mother Cindy Bostick. The Lord established that as a Church of God in Christ.

Mother Robinson had already met us when we went to Memphis in 1919, and she said to us, "You girls go forth and let the Lord use you." She gave us a letter-in those days they wasn't giving women no licenses. She gave us a letter of recommendation and with that letter of recommendation, she told us to "Go forth and help to establish churches in the Church of God in Christ," and that's what we did.

We helped establish churches all throughout the state of Missouri, throughout the state of New

Jersey, all over the United State and everyplace. In Chicago, was one of the greatest revivals that I ever conducted by myself. I didn't have my twin sister by my side, in this revival. One day, I was out on this vacant lot, bending down over an old raggedy tent and some preachers came by and saw me there. They knew me because I'd been with them in revival.

They said "Reatha, what are you doing there?" I said, "I'm patching this old raggedy tent, getting ready to have a tent meeting, in Chicago." So, I put up this tent after I had got it all fixed up and sprayed it with a solution over it that would not allow any rain in it-the preachers taught me how to put a solution on a tent that would cause it not to leak.

I put that tent up and that same night it was packed so you couldn't even get in it. I made benches with my own hands and opened up that tent that night. It was so crowded you couldn't even get in it. I carried on this great tent meeting-one of the greatest tent meetings of my career. It lasted for 30 days.

People got saved and filled with the Holy Ghost. Many of them got saved, over 300 people. Those that did get saved, got with me. I established a church there, and that church was one of the largest buildings in Chicago, because they bought a Jewish Synagogue from the Jews that were going to Jerusalem.

In this particular meeting, when I closed the meeting, the season began to get cool so I went into a building and that was where I established this church. I was in that building, still carrying on evangelism and carrying on the meeting in the building. The preachers got together in Chicago and called our Bishop Roberts, and told him, "Reatha is pastoring a church and you know the Church of God in Christ don't give women the privilege to pastor churches," and called a meeting.

Bishop Roberts had those preachers in Chicago up until three o'clock in the morning, trying to see what to do with Reatha and the church. Reatha is praying out a church. They asked me about it and I said, "I don't call it a church. I call it the evangelistic meeting and I'm still carrying on a meeting, and souls are being saved. People getting saved, all kinds of people."

Men on the street that had been living with women for years, unmarried, they got really saved and filled with the Holy Ghost. I had more young men in my service and in my building, after I went into the building, than any church in town except the Bishop's church. It was the largest in town.

They told Bishop Roberts he had to close me out and stop my meeting. He was with them until 3 o'clock in the morning-different ones talking to him.

The state supervisor was with me until three o'clock in the morning. Every once in a while, she'd punch me in the side and say, "Reatha, don't you cry. Don't you cry. God is with you. What you're doing, God is helping you do it." I didn't cry and I didn't get upset in no kind of way or feel grieved or burdened.

So, by three o'clock, all of the preachers decided- Bishop Roberts told them-that they'd "take this to Memphis and let them know what Reatha is doing here, and about the souls being saved here, and see whether they gone let her go on with it as a church or not, or what we're going to do about this."

In Memphis, it died in the Senate-that was the end of it. I never heard no more about it. They didn't bring it up in Memphis. They didn't discuss it. They didn't talk about it. Bishop Roberts told me to go on with the work. He said he was over the work his own self and if anybody caused any kind of confusion, to send them to him. That was one of the greatest accomplishments I ever had in my ministry.

They never heard one of us get up and talk about preaching. We didn't say, "God sent me to preach and I'm gonna preach- don't care what nobody say." We never did do that and don't do it today.

I believe that women today should still be careful of what they say and the words they use, that might be offensive to the church.

They should not say that they are pastoring or preaching- those are offensive words. They can save themselves some trouble if they stop saying "I am a pastor or preacher." Just do what God has given you to do-that is what Reatha and Leatha did and we stayed out of trouble.

Many years ago, I was selected by several pastors to conduct a revival in the places that they were pastoring. The first place I want to mention is in Pittsburgh, Pennsylvania where Bishop C. H. Mason, our founder, was the pastor. He told them to send and get "the girls" to carry on a revival at his church. He had several rooms over the church that he kept as an apartment for whoever carried on revival in the church.

This church was formerly pastored by T.C. Frederick, who was killed in a car accident. Bishop Mason had to take over the pastoring of that church because it was a prosperous church and well-attended. Many people were there. Bishop Mason took over that church to see after it, until he got ready to do something about that church.

During the time of waiting to get a "real" pastor there, Bishop Mason told them to send and get "the girls." In those days, they called me and my twin sister "the girls," so we carried on right there at his church. It was at that church that somebody asked us, "Now, you all say you're not preaching. Well, what are you doing?" I said, "We are doing what the mule did. God touched the mule and had him to speak in a human voice to the prophet.

God used the mule to bring the prophet to repentance. God is using me and my sister to bring sinners back to God, and you can call it what you want to call it."

The next revival that I want to mention-that God worked in a mighty way-was in Kansas City, Missouri, where V. M. Barker was the pastor. One time, his wife, Sister Barker, fell very ill. She was so sick, until the doctors gave her up to die. They thought she would never be well anymore. We were in Chicago at this time.

I had my daughter with me, who at that time was very young. I got up that morning to go to another place for a revival and God spoke to us and told us to go to Kansas City, instead of the place we thought we were going.

So early that morning, we got up out of our bed and got ready, went down to the station to go to the first place we were supposed to go to, and went up to the ticket window and asked the man about a ticket to this place. The man said, "That place is covered with water. They had a flood last night and the whole city is under water. You cannot get a train in there, today."

All at once, we had to change our direction and we came back home. My daughter asked me, "What are we doing, Mama? Where are you going? Are you going out?" I said "yes" because I had her staying with one of my sister's children, a young woman.

When I changed all at once- going to another place-my daughter laughed and said, "I thought you was going there, and you say you going to Kansas City."

I told her the Lord told us to go to Kansas City instead of this other place. We turned around, at the spur of the moment and went to Kansas City.

It was in the wintertime, the snow was almost knee-deep and very cold. Bishop Barker-Elder Barker at that time-had his church in Kansas City, Missouri and he was under all that heavy strain.

His wife was sick unto death, not expecting to get well. The church was in debt. The weather was so bad that people couldn't come out so Elder Barker could raise money to pay the bills that were due at the church. He was under awful pressure. God sent me and my twin sister there-to Kansas City-right at a time that he was under terrible distress. The Lord let a revival break out there such as we'd never had before.

People were saved, though it was very cold weather in the month of January and snow was on the ground. The church was packed every night. People came from everywhere to be in that revival. We had altar service. The altars were filled.

People were falling right and left, getting saved. God worked in a mighty, mighty way in that revival. The Lord touched the pastor's wife-that was sick unto death-and completely healed her; brought her out of that bed and put her on her feet.

We raised money enough right there-with the snow on the ground, with it being the winter time, and all odds against the pastor and the church-to pay off all the debts of the church. The Lord give us money out of that revival to pay off all the debts that were behind and healed Elder Barker's wife. We left that church on fire, shouting the victory. Many souls were added to that church. Some of those people that were saved in that revival remain there today and some of them are gone to be with the Lord. That's a revival that I will never forget how God worked in a mighty way. All odds were against us, but God got the victory.

Another time I want to mention, is in the beginning of our ministry. Bishop Crouch, Samuel Crouch, in those days was a young man on fire for God and the Lord blessed me and my sister to have favor with him. He said to us one day, "Reatha and Leatha, I want to take you to Texas and I want you to meet Bishop Mason at the Convocation."

I'd never been to Texas before in my life. It was the summertime and we went down in Waco, Texas with Bishop Crouch. He was a very famous young preacher and we went down there to be with them in the Convocation.

When we got to Waco, Bishop Crouch put us in a wagon. I've been trying to remember whether that was drawn by horses-it must have been because it was in the '20's. He put Reatha and Leatha up in a horse-drawn wagon that was truck-like and we was at the Convocation. When the people saw that he had put "those girls" up in that truck and I had my guitar and Leatha had her mandolin, and we were singing, playing and giving God the glory-the people that were in the church for the Convocation-many of them came running out to see what was going on.

Many of them were already outdoors and I will never forget, I had never been south in my life 'cause we were born in Oklahoma and there was nothing there but Indians.

I looked around to my right and my left and as far as I could see, was nothing but black people.

I've never seen that many black folks in all my life and it almost scared me. I mean, acres of them down there in Waco, Texas; just as far as you could see this way and that way, just so many of them. I said, "Lord, I didn't know that many black folks was in the world."

God raised us up there and we begin to sing and praise God. Elder Crouch went in the church somewhere and got Bishop Mason, the founder of our church. Elder Crouch told him, "I got something I want to show you there, come on and go with me," and took him out to the wagon where Reatha and Leatha was carrying on. Bishop Mason stood there and listened, and Reatha and Leatha were up in the wagon truck, carrying on for God and glorifying God.

That was when Bishop Mason said to them, "Let them girls alone, and let them carry on, and go on with whatever the Lord give them to do." So we had a great service there, out in the wagon while they were going on with the Convocation inside.

Another time I was in Detroit, Michigan when O. T. Jones was the President of the Young People's Willing Workers (YPWW) of the Church of God in Christ. He was the first that brought the words "Youth Congress" to the Church of God in Christ.

He is the one that established the Youth Congress and his son, Sammy, helped him do it. After he died, O.T. Jones Jr. took it over and carried it on until it was changed. Bishop O.T. Jones was on the inside of the building having the Youth Congress and Bishop Mason came into the Congress with him up on the platform, observing them carrying on the services.

All at once, the Lord said to me, "Go outside, Reatha and sing and pass out your ballads-your song ballads that you have composed about the World War." The World War was going on then, in 1939. That was when men were called to battle.

Ever since Pearl Harbor, our soldiers have been dying; they have died on the water; they've died on the sea and in 1939 they are dying again. That's what my song ballad was about, and I was outdoors singing that song-that men were called to battle in 1939. Somebody said, "Reatha, look up." I looked up and Bishop Mason had come out of the church and got on the roof of the porch.

That made him way up over me cause he was on the roof of the porch, and I was on the ground. He was up there just laughing, glorifying God and just enjoying me singing this song. When I found out for sure that he was there, I turned it over to him and he started preaching. We had a wonderful time. God sure got the glory.

What was the one that lived in Chicago and was saved under Reatha and Leatha-his wife, Watson-and the head man of the Sunday School? His name was Williams. Bishop Williams' wife was saved under Reatha and Leatha.

One of his daughters often talks about it. They come there and got those girls-one by one-that was saved directly under Leatha. I wasn't there, but they were saved in Evanston, Illinois in one of those revivals. That old man came there and got those women, one by one. He loved those girls to death. Never did have no trouble with them because they were saved.

Not only were men and women saved through our ministry that became bishops and state supervisors but some of them were already saved and we helped them to develop into preachers. They wasn't even no preachers, but we worked with them. The men that you hear me talk about in these various places, most all of them were touched by our ministry, somewhere. One of them who was a gambler, built five churches in Missouri. Men like that. That's right. One right now that is in Wichita, Kansas that built from the ground up three, four or five churches. He was the main man in building buildings in the last 20 years in Wichita, Kansas.

I had my hands laying right up on him and told him, "Don't give up. Hold on to God." He talks about that now; he says, "Mother had her hand on my head saying, "Hold on, hold on. Don't give up." Sho' nuff, God came through and enriched in a mighty way.

One thing that I say very humbly-that I don't know not one, I can't call one of the people that was saved directly under us that went back into the world. I can't remember not one-not one that was saved by Reatha and Leatha; they never did go back into the world-who backslid.

That is the true essence of what Holiness is all about.

One was a man who was walking the streets of Chicago, who had been living with a woman for six years-a regular sinner, living with this woman. He said she had two children. God saved him and filled him with the Holy Ghost.

He had the biggest building in Chicago and became a well-known preacher. We did that all over this country.

We carried a little tent on the train because

the people didn't know nothing about the Holy Ghost, and didn't know nothing about Pentecost.

So, when we'd go to these little towns we would hold meetings out on the corners of the street-what is called street meetings. At night, we all had little cots, and we would put them little cots down in this tent, and we'd sleep in this little tent- the twins and our oldest brother-all three of us would sleep in that tent in the night time and go out on the street in the day and hold service and teach and preach to the people about the Baptism of the Holy Ghost.

That is the very beginning of the state of Kansas hearing about the Baptism of the Holy Ghost, through the black people in those days. The people were astonished and some of them received it, and some didn't. Some fought against what we were saying and some spoke about it terrible. They thought we was all going crazy, talking in tongues and all like that, but we was just shouting and giving God the glory. So, we went on from there.

We started evangelizing, that's how we had our meetings and beat that drum and sang songs. The people would come runnin' from everywhere until maybe there would get to be 40, 50 or 100 people all around us, and then my brother started preaching about the Baptism and the Holy Ghost and we would start testifying, singing and giving God the glory.

Now, that is the beginning of Reatha and Leatha helping to get our churches-these 75 churches that you hear me talk about-in the Church of God in Christ.

The Lord blessed us to run revivals and establish churches from the east to the west coast, and everywhere in between. Many of the revivals resulted in the birthing of new churches. Other revivals brought in new souls into the kingdom of God. We ran revivals on the east coast in New York, New Jersey, Delaware, Washington D.C., Philadelphia, PA, Chicago, IL, Des Moines, IA, Lincoln, NE, Columbus, OH, Kansas City, MO, Gary, IN, and Milwaukee, WI. We ran revivals on the west coast in Pueblo, CO, Colorado Springs, CO, Albuquerque NM, Phoenix and Tucson AZ, California, Las Vegas NV, Portland, OR, and Seattle and Tacoma WA. We ran revivals in the South in Miami, FL, New Orleans, LA, Atlanta, GA, Jackson, MS, Birmingham, AL, Oklahoma City, OK, Memphis, TN and Forthworth, TX.

We went on and my brothers-not only were

they in Kansas-they went up west in the state of Colorado. There was no Church of God in Christ in Colorado, but one. He didn't have a real church.

There was one man there named Bishop Morgan. He was there but he wasn't doing no good, much. My brother went up there in Pueblo, Colorado, and started a church. That was the beginning of evangelizing in the state of Colorado. The twins went to Colorado, in time, and went around to different places with my brothers, establishing Pentecostal churches.

Now remember, at this particular time the Church of God in Christ had not organized and formulated like it did later, because nobody knew nothing about the Holy Ghost. Everybody was learning about it.

The Holy Ghost fell in 1906, and Bishop Mason came from Memphis and he received his Baptism then (in 1906). He went back to Tennessee. When he was in Tennessee, C.P. Jones and C.H. Mason were the two men that had been blessed with the Holy Ghost, but C.P. Jones did not have the Baptism of the Holy Ghost, speaking with other tongues.

When Bishop Mason went back to Tennessee, he went back to Tennessee speaking with other tongues. So Bishop Mason was speaking in tongues, and C.P. Jones was not speaking in tongues-they went to court. Bishop Samuel Crouch (with his wife) the record of that court case right now. So, I often tell young people that "speaking in tongues" went to the Supreme Court. They had to prove whether it was a cult or whether it was authentic, according to the doctrine of the Baptist and the Methodist churches-whether it was Hedonism and all like that.

It was not that, but it was a miracle. They said it was some kind of cult coming up and they wasn't like the Baptist people. Therefore, they went to C.P. Jones; he was in what they called the "Sanctified" church. Some people called them "holy jumpers." So, they went to court over speaking in tongues.

They found so many places in the Bible where they were filled with the Holy Ghost and began to speak with other tongues as the Spirit gave utterance. It was the second chapter of Acts, the 10th chapter of Acts, the 19th chapter of Acts, and all through the Bible, where they found so much speaking in tongues until the judge had to exonerate them and declare the Church of God in Christ to be an authentic religious organization.

Right now, it's registered in Washington D.C. as the Church of God in Christ. They had to go to court. The reason why they had to go to court is because they had a church building, and the building would seat-I guess-about 200 people, and both of them (Jones and Mason) had been worshiping in this building.

When Bishop Mason believed in speaking in tongues, and Bishop Jones did not believe in it, they had to separate. Somebody had to get the building and the Supreme Court gave Bishop Mason the building.

That was the beginning of the Church of God in Christ being duly recognized as an organization like any other.

CHAPTER SIXTEEN

Marriage

This is how Leatha and I became interested in getting married. My bishop said to us one day, "Reatha and Leatha, I want to see you girls get married." We was about 21 or 22 at that time.

Bishop said, "We got some fine young men here. You got to see if you can find somebody." Sure enough, I found a man named Thomas Commodore Herndon, a fiery young man-real good-looking he was. Leatha found a country boy, a cotton picker. Everybody called him the "pretty boy." He was so pretty; he was real nice looking. He looked like a Mexican.

He loved my sister. He fell in love with her and they got married. My sister said to me, "Reatha, I don't want you to be no old maid now, 'cause I'm married and I want you to marry."

That was the reason why I married. I didn't marry 'cause I wanted to marry or was crazy to marry but my sister didn't want to be married and me not married. Then my bishop wanted to see us married, too. Sho 'nuff, as time went on, we finally married these two young men and both of them didn't do right. I want to say that God didn't have nothin' to do with me marrying that man. It was not God's will at all. I married my husband in 1927. He was a popular, young preacher.

I lived with my husband about four years, as I can remember. I met Thomas Herndon in Chicago Heights, Illinois. I was introduced to him by my pastor. Two years later, we were married.

We married at W.M. Roberts's church in Chicago. Our wedding was so large that they had to block off the streets. In 1928, my husband was given a church to pastor in Chicago Heights.

My daughter was also born in 1928, in Chicago Heights. In 1929, my husband and I left his church in Chicago and traveled to Los Angeles to do evangelist work. My son was born in Los Angeles in 1930. During our marriage we were separated two or three times.

My husband started drinking. He started to run around with men and women. He was in and out of jail for lewd living. Our major and final breakup was in 1930, when my son was three months old. My husband completely drifted away from us and stayed in Los Angeles until he died in 1935, of a cerebral hemorrhage due to excessive drinking.

One of the most tragic things to happen to me in my life was losing my son. He was only three years old when he passed. I was running a revival with my sister when I received a telegram that my son was gravely ill, back home in Los Angeles. My son and daughter were being cared for by my relatives when me and my sister were conducting revivals.

When I got the telegram, I immediately caught a train to go home. When I got home, my son had just died of meningitis. This broke my heart. I never got over the loss of my son. I cry every time I talk about him. I always felt guilty about leaving my children to run revivals, but I didn't know how to do God's work and take care of my children at the same time. I now regret that I didn't stay home with my children. I am thinking now that I could have run revivals closer to home.

My daughter grew up, got her college education, even got her Master's degree and became a school principal. My daughter and I never had a real close relationship. I was not home enough to establish a good relationship with her but she grew up a good girl.

She was well-educated and she got married. She had two children. My daughter died at the age of 45, of breast cancer. I really miss her. Her son lives in back of my house right now.

Even though I know that I was doing the will of God when I was evangelizing those 75 churches and running the soul-saving revivals, I can't help but wonder about how my children may have turned out if I had spent more time with them.

I believe now that women who have been called by God to do his work and who are married with children, that their first obligation is to their husband and family. I think we have too many women who have husbands and children who are leaving them and trying to tell someone else what to do. Their house should come first; charity begins at home and spreads abroad. My husband and I didn't live together but about four years.

For some reason, the devil just completely

swept him away and caused him to lose his soul. He never did get right back to the Lord, never did. I buried him when he died, had a lovely funeral at the church for him.

Three bishops were at the funeral to bury him because he was my lawful, wedded husband and the father of my children.

Now this is Leatha's story. My sister married one month before I did, at the state Convocation in St. Louis where D. Bostic was the overseer. She met Columbus Chapman in St. Louis at the Convocation. Columbus Chapman was a cotton picker and a very country boy. He seemed to be saved to the bone. Leatha loved Columbus. He was what you call "fanatically saved." He would pick up rattle snakes because he heard the Bible say you could pick up serpents. The twins found out that he had the gift of healing. He went with Leatha on her evangelist trips. People thought he was a preacher and put him in the pulpit. Leatha had to teach him how to preach. From there, he became a preacher.

While traveling together, Leatha saw his faith and they started praying for the sick. All conditions were healed through their ministry. Their ministry and the ministry of healing caused them to go to

Detroit, Michigan where he built a famous COGIC church and became a great broadcaster.

He served in his church until he died. He became so famous that he let women separate him from Leatha. After being married for nine years, he told her one night that, "If you stay here, one of us is going to die tonight."

Leatha left that night and never went back. They did not have any children. The devil just swept those young men right from under us, out into that way of life that they chose to go.

CHAPTER FIFTEEN

Temptations

It is recorded in the Bible, in the first chapter of James, verse 15, "...when lust hath conceived, it bringeth forth sin: and sin, when it is finished, bringeth forth death."

I understood what this said when I was even young, and started out in life. My brother was 17 years old, and the twins were 4 years younger. We all had just begun to come into womanhood and manhood. We knew that the pull would be to either go one way or the other.

We would either decide to live a real strict moral life or give way to the things of the world. As I said before, we lay across the bed and solemnly swore to God that we would give our life to God. We said that we would never, never, never give way to moral decay and destruction. That very day, we swore that we would never give way to lust and immorality, drinking and all the things that go with immorality-we would never do that.

From that day, 'til this day, that was true 100 percent with me and with my brother and my sister. Leatha died-my twin sister-she died in the faith, also. So, we thank God that He took us through many temptations that were given to us, offered to us, to take us down; to bring down our moral standards; but we refused.

It seems to me that sometimes, the Holy Ghost would stand up in me as big as a mule, against sexual degradation and I would live to the course of a clean, spotless life.

Mother Coffey, during her lifetime, used to walk across the floor, and would be shaking her finger as she would say, "These girls have walked in this church for many, many years-spotless and have lived for the Lord." She was glad and gloried in the standards we'd taken for the Lord. We believed in peace with all men, and "...holiness, without which no man shall see the Lord," (Heb 12:14). We believed that, we lived it and we stood for it and Mother Coffey was glad that we did.

Well, I think I told you about the young man that seemed like he loved me and I thought that I liked him or loved him or something. He asked me to run away with him and get married. Many, many times I have been tempted. I've even had preachers come to my house and try their best to get me to go to bed with them and I'd tell them, "I don't do that. I don't do that." See, I said to God years ago, that I would never stoop to immorality and I never have.

I married as a virgin. We had two children. My husband packed up his clothes one day. He left me when my baby boy was three months old. When my husband and I split up, I never had another man. I never married again. I lived a saved life from that day to this one.

CHAPTER SEVENTEEN

I am Making an Example Out of You

I found out later in life, that there are right now seven things, handicapping, hindering and afflicting me-seven different afflictions on me. But I'm glad that God said through all afflictions, He would bring us through.

The first affliction is with my eyes. Secondly, about 10 or 11 years ago, in my bedroom I was going around the foot of my bedroom and I had a fall. When I fell, I didn't have no idea it had hurt me very much, but I couldn't get up. I turned over on my hands and knees-off of my back-and crawled to the living room and pulled myself up on the sofa. I didn't feel that I had really hurt myself very bad but every day after that it began to get worse and worse.

Come to find out after I had this fall, about two weeks after, the misery and the conditions got unbearable so they took me to the hospital. When they carried me to White Memorial Hospital in Los Angeles, the doctor x-rayed my hip and diagnosed the condition of my hip. It was broke in three places. He said to me, "Mrs. Herndon, do you know your hip is broke in three places? We're gonna have to put a steel rod in your hip." They put me to sleep and I didn't know nothing about it.

They operated on my hip, pinned me back together and put me in my room to recover. One thing I want to thank God for, it never did give me no real pain or real worry about my hip. Though I couldn't turn over, they made a scaffold over my bed for me to pull up by, to use the bedpan. I couldn't get up until this rod had taken effect. That took 30 days. I was out 30 days in the hospital for this rod to be set up- as it should be-and I'd be able to get up and walk again.

From that time, until now I remain a cripple. When I got ready to leave the hospital, they put me learning how to walk again, and walking with a walker. From that, they gave me a wheelchair as

I left the hospital and I'm in a wheelchair today. That's been more than 10 years ago. That's number two. My eyesight is gone and I'm crippled in my hip.

The next thing that happened to me is my ears got so I couldn't hear very well. Right now, I can't hear very well, insomuch as I can't understand what the preacher is saying when he's preaching, and when people are talking to me I can't understand what they're saying very well. That's a great handicap and that's three.

My eyes, crippled and my ears. After I had the terrible fall over 10 years ago, arthritis set in, right afterwards. That was the thing that has kept me in a wheelchair for these 10 years.

Right now, I cannot stand up long, cannot walk to amount to anything because arthritis has made me a cripple. For some reason, a deadness came in both my hands and fingers, only the fingers, not the whole hand. I couldn't pick up nothing, I can't button my clothes, I can't handle nothing. All the feeling is out of my fingers and they all became like wood.

So, I had these things happen to me and I asked the Lord, "Why is it that I have all these afflictions that is rendering me to almost be a helpless cripple and not able to go nowhere, stand up and do things that I've been doing all my life, and yet I have all this work to do for you?"

The answer came back, "I am making an example out of you. I'm making an example out of you and I'm showing the world-through you being afflicted like you are-you're still going on, you haven't let nothing hinder you from making trips.

For instance, since you've been cripple you've been as far as Boston, Massachusetts, from Los Angeles. You've been as far south as Tampa, Florida. You've been many times as far as Memphis, Tennessee, and all around. You cannot let nothing hinder you.

And I wanted to prove to the world that there is such a thing as to know God as a Healer, to know God as a Provider, to know God as a Conqueror, to know God as a Helper, to help you over hurdles, regardless of what they are. You have kept on going to show the world that it can be done. I wanted to manifest Myself through you, so I have made you an example." When the Lord said that to me-in my heart-I said, "Thank you Jesus. I'm willing for You to make an example out of me on the airplanes, in the trains, in the automobiles, or wherever I go."

When I bring a message, they sit down a chair by the side of the pulpit and I bring the message from the platform, but in a chair. Sometimes the Lord sets the whole church on fire and the glory of the Lord comes down and many people are saved and blessed through the message, regardless of me being crippled and being so disabled-God gets the glory.

That's why He told me, "I'm making an example out of you that you may know Him in the power of His resurrection and be confirmed in the image of His Son."

I want to thank God for being as well as I am. One of the things I thank God for is-concerning my health-that I don't feel sick. I don't feel worn out in my body or broke down in my body. My mind is as keen as it can be and all of the pastors where I go and serve, they all marvel at the wisdom and how God is able to deliver the message through having a good memory at 101 years old. I will be 101 years old October 11, 2001. So, God told me, "That's the reason I want to make an example out of you."

Leatha & Reatha

They preached in the sunshine, rain and snow. They fearlessly went into these areas and established numerous churches throughout the nation. They embodied the true essence of the Great Commission of Jesus Christ which says in Matthew 28:19, *"Go ye therefore, and teach all nations, baptizing them in the name of the Father, and of the Son, and of the Holy Ghost."*

Your Servant in Christ,
Bishop Charles E. Blake Sr.,

The Seventh in Succession
The Presiding Bishop
The Church Of God in Christ, Inc.

"God told me...

"That's the reason I want to make an example out of you."

- Mother Reatha Herndon

Let God Make An Example Of You, Too!

- Doris J. Sims

Made in the USA
Charleston, SC
01 November 2014